Dreaming in English

A Memoir

Jeannie Johng-Nishikawa

Requests for permission to reproduce material from this work
should be sent to jjohngnishikawa@gmail.com

Published by West River Publishing
2744 Del Rio Place, Suite 210
Davis, CA 95618
United States

Extended Edition
ISBN 979-11-950324-4-0

Printed in the Republic of South Korea

Book Cover Design by Prerna Dudani
Author's photograph © by Stephen Anthony

Dreaming in English

A Memoir

Jeannie Johng-Nishikawa

Extended Edition

Table of Contents

Dreaming
in English
A Memoir

Part II **America**

Foreword by Wayne Maeda

As an educator for over 40 years in Asian American Studies, I instantly recognized the value of this memoir. In *Dreaming in English: A memoir*, Jeannie Johng-Nishikawa tells a highly accessible, engaging, insightful, multilayered, and timely story of her family's poverty-stricken life during the post-Korean War era and their struggles and triumphs in what they thought would be heaven on earth, America. *Dreaming in English*, is a timely story helping us, the millions of Asians and other immigrants who have and continue to arrive in America, understand life's challenges.

Beginning in 1965, immigration laws for Eastern Hemisphere countries put them on a more equal footing with Western Hemisphere countries. These changes in immigration laws allowed 20,000 to emigrate from each Asian country. U.S. involvement in a war in Southeast Asia, and the addition of various categories of sponsorship all accounted for eye-popping growth. This trend towards increasing growth and diversity of Asian Americans continues to this day. Preliminary findings of the 2010 U.S. Census indicate that persons of Asian ancestry make up 5.6 percent of the total U.S. population. The Chinese are the largest group, with about 3.8 million, followed by 3.4 million Filipino, 3.2 million Asian Indian, 1.7 million Vietnamese, 1.7 million Korean, and 1.3 million Japanese. With all this growth and arrival of new immigrants, *Dreaming in English* will be relevant for many years to come.

While these are indeed diverse groups coming to America, Jeannie and her family's experiences both in Korea and in America are told simply and honestly from the point of view a third daughter in a family of eight (five siblings, mother, and father). Her story is, in many ways unique, but it is also a universal story of immigrants and refugees who have come from all over the world to America. Jeannie's experiences of discovering her first refrigerator, not speaking or understanding English, and licking her first mint chocolate chip ice cream cone can resonate with both old and new immigrants, whether they crossed an ocean that they never knew existed or encountered indoor running hot water and toilets 100 years ago.

Even more important, Jeannie's story is a universal one. Families must navigate their way through the maze of deep clashes of culture, generation, race, gender, class, and ultimately finding one's own identity and voice in their place of settlements. Ultimately, Jeannie's story is about finding her own voice and balancing her life in two worlds, a story every young person can relate to.

Dreaming in English is a "must read" and can be used in a variety of settings:

For teachers who work with culturally and linguistically diverse students this memoir provides insights into the difficulties of adjusting to an alien cultural and language acquisition as well subverting the Asian American stereotypes of the "Model Minority" and "Tiger Mother," reminding us that not all "Asians" are alike and to view and teach each student as an individual.

For students who are struggling to learn a new language and confronting issues of cultural conflicts, this memoir is highly accessible and will no doubt provides them with a template to share their own experiences with fellow classmates, and perhaps encourage them to seek and find their own voice.

For counselors and service providers working with any diverse population, Jeannie's story is a reminder that bullying and clashes of culture, class, gender, and race can have a huge impact on one's life chances and academic achievements.

For the rest of us, *Dreaming in English* is a poignant reminder of the resiliencies and life-affirming qualities that many newcomers bring and why they still want to come to America. Equally insightful, especially in these xenophobic times, is the impact that ordinary people can have on newcomers through acts of individual kindness and speaking up on their behalf as they make the transition to dreaming in English or a combination of languages.

▪ Wayne Maeda, Lecturer Emeritus, Ethnic Studies (1947 – 2013)

▪ California State University, Sacramento

Author's Note

I first became inspired to write this story for my three children, Ryan, Victoria and Thomas. My husband and I would read to them almost every night, usually the same books, time after time. Eventually, I got tired of reading the same stories, and so one night I decided to give them a personal narrative about what my life was like growing up on a farm in South Korea. The children loved it and asked to hear more details. Their enthusiasm prompted me to write it down in a yellow spiral notebook including sketches and illustrations.

My friend, Dr. Romana Norton, came over for lunch and spotted my yellow notebook. She asked if she could read it, but I had always been embarrassed about my writing. It took some friendly coaxing, but I eventually let her take a look. She liked my story and insisted I keep writing. With her encouragement, I continued writing for two years. Along the way, I became discouraged and even quit momentarily. Then in August of 2009, when Umma (my mother) was diagnosed with stage-four lung cancer, I was motivated to write again.

I've always wanted to give Umma something special since she dedicated her life to giving my siblings and me everything we needed. I decided I would finish this book for her, whether it would be published or not.

With the help of Dr. Michelle (Chungyeol) Park, I was able to publish the first edition in April of 2011.

My hope is that this book carries some of Umma's spirit, and the story resonates with my readers.

When I was a child, the voices of my dreams spoke in Korean. When I became an American, the Korean voices left me, and my dreaming voices found their new language.

For Umma, Chun Ku Yi (1942 – 2015)

And for my three children: Ryan, Victoria, and Thomas

Acknowledgments

I want to thank my three children: Ryan, Victoria, and Thomas. You teach me to love something new every day. Nothing is more important to me than spending time with each one of you.

And to my husband, Rod Nishikawa, for your love and patience.

My endless gratitude extends to my five siblings, Jin-sun (Jennifer Ng), Jin-bok (Sandra Chong-Walker), Jin-hun Chong, Jeong-mi (Lisa Ohara), and Jin-suk (Jenny Allen) for your unwavering support.

And to Appa (Father) for doing what you could to support us despite of your lack of formal education. Even though you weren't around much, I know you were out there toiling on whatever work you could find to feed us and give us a place to live.

Holly Asano—you are an amazing lady. You've been

like a second mother to me and a third grandmother to my children. Thank you for your endless hours over the years, loving my children, reading to them, and playing with them. Thank you for caring for my family in sickness and in health. You are always available at a moment's notice, even at two o'clock in the morning.

There are so many people who helped make this book happen. They are the following: Dr. Shin Dong-Ae, Dr. Eom Doo-yong, Dr. Kim Tae Kyeong, Dr. Shin Dong-eun, Lee Kang-hoon, Dr. Yoon In-jin at Korea University, Lee Hyun-jun at the Foreign Ministry in Seoul, Korea, my late uncle Kwon Oh-koon, Dr. James Housefield from the University of California at Davis, Dr. Heather Sellens from California State University, Sacramento, and Heather Caswell for suggesting the title for this book.

I have to thank Jennifer Thompson, Drs. Karen and Bill Vernau, and Karen Ruan for watching my children so that I could write and finish this book. Thank you for all those play dates.

I also want to thank Doug, Carleen, and Amanda McDavid for being a part of my life and my children's lives for so many years.

I am so grateful to Dr. Michelle (Chungyeol) Park at Korea Nazarene University for translating my book from English into Korean and for helping me to publish this book in Korea. Thank you for believing in me.

Special thanks to Kiik Araki-Kawaguchi, Morton Rumberg, Ken Umbach, Mallory Sellens, and Younghee Her.

I am extremely blessed to know all of you. I will do my best to return your love and support for the rest of my life. May God be with you and bless you all the days of your life. Thank you!–Jeannie (September 15, 2014).

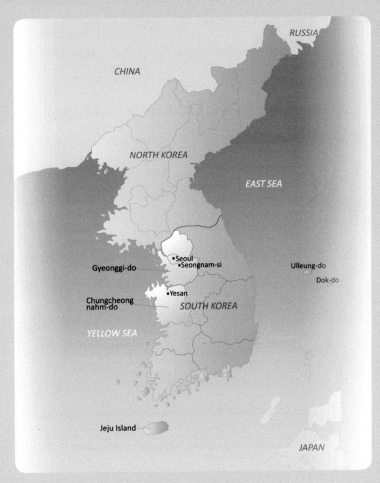

Map of Korea where Sami lived with her family.

Part I Korea

Dreaming
in English
A Memoir

Chapter 1

Life on the Farm

My name is Sami. I was born in the spring of 1968, the year of the Monkey, in Yesan, Chungcheongnahm-do, South Korea. I was born on a farm and lived with my father, Appa, my mother, Umma, my brother, Jin-hun, and my sisters, Jin-sun, Jin-bok, Jeong-mi, and Jin-suk. I am the third daughter and middle child. My birth marked fifteen years since the end of the Korean War and twenty-three years since the Japanese occupiers finally left Korea.

Park Jeong-hee was the President of Korea at that time and the third President of South Korea overall. The conditions in South Korea had improved by the late sixties, but it was very difficult to make a living in farming areas like the village where we lived. Since not everyone ate three meals a day, an education was not as important in Chungcheongnahm-do as having a full stomach.

When Appa suggested sending his younger brother to Seoul for schooling, my Halmoni (paternal grandmother) relayed to him, "Education is not going to feed you when you are hungry. It is more important to live for today than to live for tomorrow because tomorrow might not come."

My Halmoni knew what it felt like to be hungry for days, not knowing when or where she was going to see her next meal. She survived Japan's brutal colonization of Korea when she was a teenager only for her first husband to die tragically. His unexpected death left Halmoni a young widow with five children all under the age of eleven. Shortly thereafter, World War II commenced.

From 1945 to 1950, South Koreans were so poor and hungry that many had signed their names with their wooden stamps to show their allegiance to the communist party just so that they could receive a free bag of rice. They did not fully understand the consequences at the time, which led to entire families killed for being communists.

When I was four years old, Umma was pregnant with her fifth child. During this time, Appa had to close down his coal mining business in Yesan, Chungcheonnahm-do and move the family to another small farm village, Seongnam-si, Gyeonggi-do. This village was about twenty miles south of Seoul, and I would call it home for the next six years. I rarely traveled outside my village and never knew it was so close to a major city as I lived by several mountains, rivers, and lakes. During the Korean War (1950 – 1953), most of the pine trees surrounding my village were chopped down for building homes and for heating. Following the war, more trees were planted and subsequently everywhere I turned, new pine trees stretched over the landscape for miles and miles.

You could see red, blue, and gray tile roofs in my new village, but our home had rice straw for roofing, just like we'd had back in Yesan. Though these types of roofs didn't last long, they provided warmth in the winter and kept the house cool in summer. They were also less expensive, which led Umma to decide on straw roofing as we could not afford tile roofing at the time.

Seongnam-si, Gyeonggi-do was a beautiful and peaceful village, surrounded by a series of small mountains. There was a long river used by everyone in our village for farming, washing clothes, swimming, sledding, and ice fishing. We had no telephone, television, or automobile as we did not see any of these inventions until 1977. Although we left for America when I was only ten, I remember Korea being a peaceful place; however, my parents only remember

Korea as a place of backbreaking work and little else.

All I remember of Yesan was my visits to my Halmoni. Whenever I visited her, I wore bright, new clothes in a variety of colors and carried a small umbrella with me. When I arrived, my sahm-chohn (my paternal uncle) would give me shoulder rides. Every time I went outside of Halmoni's house to look up at the mountains, she would exclaim, "Sami, don't go up there. If you do, the tiger is going to eat you." I never forgot that. Nights were hard at Halmoni's with the unsetting sounds of howling wolves filling the night air. They were so loud and felt so close. With the exception of my time with Halmoni, other memories of my birthplace are blurry.

It wasn't until much later that I found out why my older sister, Jin-bok, could not go with me to visit Halmoni. Jin-bok was born in 1966, the year of the White Horse, which comes every sixty years. It is considered a good omen for boys to be born in the year of the White Horse; however, for girls, it signifies bad luck. Appa and Halmoni did not hold or touch Jin-bok from the first day of her life on this earth. She never received any love from either of them. The only love she received was from Umma. Jin-bok grew up tough and cold. She had freckles on her face and darker skin than most of us. This was another bad omen since Korean girls were supposed to have clear, cream-colored skin.

Today, Jin-bok possesses a loud, deep voice that could pass for that of a man. She has unusually large, round eyes with eyelashes as long as the Han River, which is unusual for Korean girls. I think she is beautiful and her strength reminds me of a black stallion.

Halmoni never hid the fact that she disliked Jin-bok. She was always saying things like, "Look at her-she has dark skin! She is bad luck! I don't want to see her! Don't bring her to my house!" As she proclaimed these thoughts to Umma so many times, I was sure Jin-bok heard this as well.

Halmoni also disliked Jin-bok because Umma had a stillborn boy in her sixth month of pregnancy before becoming pregnant and giving birth to Jin-bok. Appa and Sahm-chohn buried my deceased brother shortly after Umma gave birth to him. Halmoni never got over his death and always blamed Jin-bok for it.

In addition, Halmoni blamed Umma for everything that went wrong with Appa's life. Umma gave birth to five healthy girls; however, Halmoni claimed that girls were useless. She often said Umma was cursed, which is why she gave birth to so many girls. Halmoni always lectured, "Boys good luck; girls bad luck."

When Umma finally gave birth to my brother Jin-hun, Halmoni was happy. Umma still says to us girls that Jin-hun is worth more than five daughters put together. However, my feelings aren't hurt as I can't even imagine what Umma must have felt to have so many daughters and so few sons. Halmoni let me come over to her house only after my brother was born. She said that I was good luck for having a younger brother. But still, Jin-bok was never allowed to come to Halmoni's home.

Chapter 2

Before the Farm

Around the time my brother was born, Appa's coal mining business went under. He had sold his last small plot of land in Chungcheonnahm-do in order to start his business, only for it to fail after eighteen months.

At one time, Appa possessed more land, but sold it to help his young brother, Joon-mo, who was having financial difficulties. My uncle Joon-mo was constantly asking Appa for money. It was common practice in Korean culture to give siblings money even if it meant both of you would eventually go under. Uncle Joon-mo took Appa's money and started a small business selling rice popcorn. It failed quickly, so he came to

31

Appa for more money. This time, Appa couldn't help him until his three-year commitment to the army was over as soldiers did not receive any pay. The allowance he received from the Korean government was only 1300 won ($1.30) per month. To offset his low income, Appa received free haircuts, three meals a day, uniforms, and a place to sleep for his service.

While Appa was serving in the Korean Army, Umma and Unni survived by eating rice and vegetables a local farmer grew for my family on the land that Appa owned. The farmer took half of the crops for his pay.

Umma kept herself and my older sister warm during winter by burning straw when they ran out of wood. My family was one of the lucky ones since many soldiers did not own their own land.

In 1964, Appa finished serving in the military and his older sister, Sun-mo, helped him start his mining business. His sister lived in America, and they were very close. My grandfather passed away when Appa was only seven, and Sun-mo was eleven. After Appa's father, Harabaji, passed away, Halmoni was never there for her five children from her first marriage. She told them to look for their own food and money. Halmoni did not even help Appa start his business.

Before he began mining, Appa didn't research the mountain to see if it had coal. Instead, he relied upon the word of people who lived outside of our province. Appa sold his small plot to buy mining equipment only to find that the mountain had no coal, and without the capital to pay his workers, he had to close.

Appa was a proud and optimistic man. Since he never liked farming, he was hopeful that he could make it big with a business venture. But after the mine closed, Appa had to move out of Chungcheongnahm-do to save face.

Chapter 3

Sweet Potatoes and Watermelons

It was wonderful that Appa and Umma had so many children on the farm. In spring and summer, our family grew everything we ate for the year. We couldn't afford to buy food. We harvested our own rice, wheat, barley, sweet potatoes, lettuce, watermelons, *cham-weh* (Korean melon), garlic, leeks, onions, chives, Napa cabbages, cucumbers, squash, eggplants, soybeans, and radishes.

Umma planted a lot of sweet potatoes. They were red on the outside and orange-yellow on the inside, and when the sweet potatoes were cooked, they were even sweeter. Umma cooked the sweet potatoes four different ways. Sometimes, she would cut the sweet potatoes into half-inch cubes and throw them into the pot of rice right before the rice was finished cooking while other times, she would boil them in a large pot. On occasion, she steamed the sweet potatoes, making them taste like chestnuts. During the winter months, she often roasted them over the fire in the kitchen that also heated the one bedroom we used for living, playing, sewing, studying, and sleeping.

On the west facing side of our home, there was a storefront where Umma cooked for people on occasion. Some of our neighbors liked Umma's cooking, and they came to eat and pay for the food. It was like a restaurant. When we didn't have any customers, we used the storefront to play in. During the winter months, we would eat our sweet potato snacks, and Umma would cut our hair there.

When Umma planted sweet potatoes, the ground had to be soft and tilled. She cut the potatoes into small pieces with one or two eyes around them. Next, Umma planted the pieces of potato inside the ground about five or six inches apart from one another and cover them with dirt. She watered them until the sweet potatoes were ready to be harvested around twelve weeks later. As sweet potato leaves were green on the top and greenish-purple on the bottom, they looked like ivy leaves.

When the sweet potatoes were ready to be harvested, Umma would carefully dig them out of the ground, leaving them on top of the tilled dirt for Jin-bok and me to collect them. We were always so surprised how one small piece of a sweet potato could produce so many individual potatoes. The potatoes weren't consistent in size, yet they were all delicious when we ate them. Their size didn't detract from their mellow and roasted taste.

Growing our crops was not an easy task. We did not have an irrigation system. Umma had to carry the water from the creeks, rivers, and mountains near our fields. It was hard work, but luckily, the water was free, and there was plenty of it.

Umma had to work hard so her children had enough food to eat in the fall and enough to store for the winter and spring. During springtime, Umma got up early everyday to plant and do housework. Sometimes, she would lament to me, "This life is just too hard. I've thought of killing myself, but I can't do it because I promised my mother that I would stay married to your Appa until death. Plus, I can't imagine leaving my children behind." This sentiment was closely followed by her proclaiming, "I would sell everything I have, but I will never give up on my children as long as I'm alive."

Though our family was poor, Umma felt very rich because she had six children who made her smile and laugh every day. She said her mother once told her never to worry about how many children she had as

God would provide each child with just enough to live on this earth. Umma did not pray, but she believed in God, which made her feel confident about her life. Even when she was discouraged. She never worried about not having enough food on the table or enough clothing for her children. When the food was running short during the winter months, and we only had *jook* (rice porridge), she persevered, taking care of her six children one day at a time.

Despite all the difficult work Umma had to do around the farm, she still had time for discipline. Once, when Jin-bok and I were bickering, my mother lectured me about respecting my sister and not arguing with her as she was older. However, when one of my younger sisters, Jeong-mi, was arguing with me, Umma instructed me not to argue with her because she was younger. Anger washed over me. I confronted Umma and asked her, "Why are you only telling me to give up the argument and not Jin-bok or Jeong-mi?" She answered, "I know you are the one who will listen to me and stop arguing." I was upset with Umma at the time, but later, I realized she understood her children well. Today I thank her for her wisdom.

Umma taught me how to love my siblings unconditionally. To this day, I thank Umma for giving me a sweet brother and four beautiful sisters, who will be my friends for life. I expressed to Umma that giving me my siblings was more precious than any amount of money or education. We may not always get along, but my brother and my sisters support me in anything I do in my life. I will always love them, no matter what happens.

Umma taught us life lessons by speaking to us in parables. Once she asked me, "Does fresh water come from the mountain or the ocean," and I informed her, "Of course, the mountain."

I got bothered with her for asking such a foolish question. However, she wouldn't get upset with me, instead claiming that I was the mountain and my younger siblings were the ocean. Just as the fresh water flowed from the mountain to the ocean, so would my actions, thus affecting my younger siblings. When I stopped to think about what she was saying, I knew Umma was right.

We had only a few acres of land to grow all our food and used every square foot to grow vegetables, fruits, and grains. No space was wasted. My family woke up very early in the morning before the sun rose, and went to bed late at night. Umma did most of the farming, but when my two eldest sisters and I got older, we helped her around the farm. She also sewed, knitted, cooked, cleaned, washed clothes in the river, and gathered wild herbs, all while taking care of her six young children.

For me and my siblings, it was not always hard work on the farm. Sometimes, Umma told us to go outside and play with other children in our village.

Most of the time, however, we played among ourselves because there were six of us at home. When my sister Jin-bok and I got bored, we went outside near the creeks and rivers to pick wild herbs called *suk* (mugwort) for Umma. She would use *suk* as medicine to treat infections, but mostly she used it in our food. She would make us *suk* soup and *suk boochimgae*, a type of pancake. *Suk* was also used to make dyes for fabrics and for food coloring.

Down by the creeks, we also built a playhouse. We would take large rocks and stack them up as high as possible, building three-sided walls and pretending that it was our home. When we got hungry after playing all day, we would go look for Umma.

Umma would put a couple of large, ripe watermelons on the edge of the river early in the day to keep them cold. She knew which watermelons were ripe by knocking on the side of them a few times with her fist. If they sounded hollow, they were ready, so Umma would place a few rocks around the watermelons to prevent them from rolling downstream. In those days, no one had a cooler. After Umma worked all day in the fields, she would come down to the river where we played and cut the watermelons in small slices to us. We ate as many slices as we wanted, gorging ourselves until we couldn't eat anymore. They were so sweet and cold. When we bit into them, they melted in our mouths. The best part of eating the watermelons was the black seeds in our mouths. With our legs dangling in the cold river, we would see who could spit them the farthest.

Chapter 4

Thirsty Cow

The summer of 1972 was hot and muggy on the farm. Umma had to go out in the fields to tend to the crops and give water to our chickens and our cow. The cow, which we borrowed from Halmoni, was light brown in color and had short, soft fur. She had the prettiest eyes with eyelashes that reached the heavens. Like Halmoni, our cow had a stubborn nature.

When Umma went to check on the animals in the morning, she noticed Halmoni's cow wasn't eating or drinking. She checked on the cow again after lunch, but still, the cow would not eat or drink. Umma was concerned as the cow wasn't sick from what she observed. Umma explained to me, "Sami, if this cow won't eat or drink, we won't have any milk or any help tilling the soil."

Umma tied the cow beneath the shade of a nearby tree not far from our field, and the cow stood there all day. Umma could sense the cow was weak and thirsty, but when she brought the cow water, she refused to drink. Umma kept her tied to the tree into the early evening. She put sea salt in the water jug in an effort to increase thirst. Fortunately, when Umma approached her later that evening, the cow quickly and desperately drank. Perhaps the cow was so thirsty that she didn't notice the sea salt. Later, Umma brought out fresh food and drink for the cow, and this time, she had no qualms about eating and drinking.

After that day, the cow never refused a meal, and as she ate so well, she provided plenty of milk. The milk was warm and sweet with the consistency of cream. She also plowed for us after the harvest, so Umma could get the field ready for planting the following spring. Eventually, we had to return her to Halmoni, but the cow worked hard for us during that short period.

I guess she wasn't as stubborn as Halmoni after all.

Chapter 5

Frog Legs

During our childhood, Jin-bok and I spent a lot of time playing outside. There was plenty of open space to explore in the countryside and we could run in any direction and not see a single house. The sky was deep blue and the warm air caressed our faces, filling our nostrils with the smell of pungent wildflowers. Most days we didn't wear shoes, feeling the delicate earth under our small feet.

The summer months were the best time to be outside because the trees and plants were green and flourishing with life. There were so many different insects too. When the sun set, beautiful fireflies blinked on and off in the dark of the night. During the day, we could see thousands of yellow-brown grasshoppers in the rice fields. Jin-bok and I would catch grasshoppers in a clear jar and take them to Umma and she would roast them for snacks. We did this before Appa and Umma cut down the ripe rice straw with machetes as the grasshoppers would flee from our field to another until everything was harvested in our village.

During summer and early fall, we also ate frog legs. Jin-bok and I would go out into the creeks along the rice fields and catch frogs for Umma. Jin-bok was very brave. She would jump into the creek and search for frogs while I would wait on the bank. Then she would hand me the frogs after she caught them from the bottom of the creek bed, and I would put them in a large can with a lid. I didn't like catching frogs because I thought they were ugly, slimy, and slippery. They were gray-black on top and white on their bellies and were usually between four and six inches long. The frogs knew to quickly jump away from us, but Jin-bok was incredibly fast. If I had ever managed to catch one frog, she would have already caught several.

With our can full of frogs, we rushed home to Umma. Jin-bok and I watched excitedly as Umma cleaned and separated the frog legs from the bodies with one clean stroke of the knife, throwing the bodies away. She washed and peeled the skin and seasoned the legs with salt, pepper, garlic, and green onions. She also used a hot red pepper sauce she'd made using peppers from our garden. The legs were cooked in a pan with sesame seed oil, bringing a wonderful aroma to our home. We harvested our own sesame seeds to make the sesame oil in those days, as it was the only oil we could afford on our small farm.

Sometimes instead of frying them, Umma would boil the frog legs in a large pot of hot and spicy soup. Appa liked the soup hot and spicy. Umma always tried to make him happy since he was still depressed that his coal mining operation had gone out of business. During those times, we could not afford beef or pork, so instead we ate plenty of frog legs and fish.

Umma told me that in those days, she was very concerned about my health. She recalled I was always slow getting to the table and since my siblings ate faster than I did, I grew incredibly skinny. Umma began to hide food from my siblings for me to eat later. She thought if she fed me enough frog legs, I would gain weight and stay healthy. I never did gain any weight, but I remember eating a plethora of frog legs with rice and the vegetable dishes Umma made from our farm crops. The frog legs were sweet and spicy as Umma heavily seasoned them for me with garlic, onions, and red pepper to mask any smell I didn't like.

To this day, Umma hides portions of food for me during our family dinners in an effort to make me gain weight.

Chapter 6

Catching a Snake

In September 1973, I went with Umma to check our crops in the small, sweet potato field. It was warm in the morning, and the fall harvest was just around the corner. The rice field was a golden yellow and looked ready to be picked. Grasshoppers were jumping from one plant to the next, happily looking for rice on the parts of the plant that were still green.

On the right side of the field, our sweet potato plants grew beautifully. The leaves covered the field, so we couldn't see any part of the ground after planting the potatoes. I was always afraid to step into the field as I couldn't tell what was lurking under the plants, thus I stayed away as much as I could. As I was catching the yellowish-brown grasshoppers, I heard a loud scream from the sweet potato field where Umma was working. I turned to see what was happening only to find Umma scared and immobile.

Umma told me not to come any closer for she saw a gray-black snake. She had accidentally stepped on it, and it had jumped into the air. It landed near her and was hiding somewhere beneath the sweet potato leaves. Umma did not want either of us to be bitten. She grabbed a thick rod with her dark, withered hands and went to search for the snake. "Sami, stay far away from the sweet potato plants until I catch the snake," Umma warned with a grave tone.

She was very brave. I wanted to run away, but she said to me, "Sami, if we don't catch this snake today, it might bite one of us or someone else tomorrow." She took the rod and carefully walked up and down the sweet potato rows until she located the snake. It was trying to be still, but Umma was faster and smarter. She walked toward the snake without making any noise. Circling around it, Umma hit the snake on its head several times until she was sure it was unconscious. She then tied a thin strip of tree bark around its mouth and wrapped the gray-black snake around the rod. Umma and I walked toward the village where our family lived. It was about half a mile away on an unpaved road. While Umma and I walked in the center of the road, the snake had wrapped itself around the rod and was playing dead. I was still feeling shocked that Umma had caught it. Suddenly, Umma seemed so much bigger and stronger to me.

People gathered around as we got closer to the village. They were amazed to see a small woman like Umma with such a large and long snake. Umma was supposed to be a lady. She was from the *yangban* class (noble woman). Most people in our village knew about Umma and her background. They knew she came from a huge Yi family in Yesan, Chungcheongnahm-do. Her family had a written history dating back over eight hundred years. Umma had her own servants until the first of March 1959 when she and Appa were married in an arranged marriage.

People in our village were surrounding Umma and asking if she would sell the snake to anyone, but she refused. She brought the snake home to her small kitchen and poured vodka into a deep, narrow, and clear glass bottle before washing the snake. After washing it, she put the snake into the clear glass bottle, tail first. She released the bark from the snake's head and quickly pushed it into the narrow opening, drowning the snake in vodka. While watching her prepare the snake in the kitchen, I was afraid of the two of them. As humans and snakes are natural enemies, I was surprised to see Umma act without fear.

Umma kept the snake in that clear glass bottle for many years. Whenever she had a friend with an ailment, she gave him or her a drink. However, most people, including myself, were too afraid to try it.

In 1986, Umma brought the snake with her to the United States from Korea after originally leaving it with one of her cousins. The jarred snake was wrapped in a dark cloth and put in her suitcase to get it through customs. To this day, she still keeps it in her refrigerator.

Chapter 7

Yangban Burial Process

When I turned seven in August 1975, I remember that it was blistering hot and humid, and especially so on days following rain. Umma was pregnant with my youngest sister, Jin-suk. She was growing larger, heavier, and wearier by the day, but continued to rise early to tend to the farm and care for five children. Often, I went to the fields with Umma, and on our way we chatted with our neighbors. Under Umma's protection, I felt safe. In general, I was shy, but around Umma, I felt outgoing.

One morning, as we were walking toward the bridge near our field, I saw a group of people around

Mr. Kim's home. Mr. Kim, Harabaji, as I called him, smoked a pipe and had gray hair with a long gray-white mustache with a sharp point at the end of it. As his back was bent, he was forced to walk with a cane, which made him look shorter. Umma told me to call him Harabaji, meaning "grandpa," to show him proper respect since he was one of the oldest men in our village.

When we arrived at Mr. Kim's home, we sensed something tragic had occurred as forlorn faces surrounded the property. Deciding not to go to the fields that day, we turned into Mr. Kim's courtyard and were told that he had passed away. In the mist of their sobs, people in his courtyard were serving food and drinks to the guests who had stopped by to pay their respects. Nearly everyone in our village was involved with Mr. Kim's funeral. Seongnam-si was such a small village, and it seemed as though everyone was related to Mr. Kim.

I had never seen a dead person or attended a funeral in my life. I wanted to see what Harabaji looked like, but Umma wouldn't let me. I was curious and scared about death at the same time. This was the first time I realized that life had an end; Umma and Appa would die, and I too would die eventually. I wanted to know where Harabaji had gone. Umma relayed to me, "Sami, after our loved ones die, they sail to an afterlife on a boat. That is why our family packs food so that they have some on their journey to the next life."

Umma had witnessed her aunt's burial ceremony during the summer of 1965. Umma's aunt, whom everyone called "Keun Umma," was married to Umma's paternal uncle, who died of old age in the late 1950s. Keun Umma was one of the elders in the family and made many decisions regarding women's issues, like who would marry whom and when their marriages would take place. She taught the women and young granddaughters how to cook, weave, embroider blankets and pillows, and iron sheets and clothing by pounding them with two rounded wooden rods. She also taught them proverbs. From the *yangban* (noble) family of *Chea-si*, she was a wise and kind lady and all the women, men, and grandchildren in the Yi family household looked up to her for her wisdom. When she passed away, everyone was shocked and upset.

Her body needed to be cleaned and posed within a couple of hours before rigor mortis set in. As soon as she passed away, the elder aunts gathered the family into the bedroom in order to show them how to perform the *yangban* burial process from start to finish.

The process commenced with undressing Keun Umma. Several female servants brought clean hand towels and warm water in two small bowls. One of the younger aunts closed both of Keun Umma's eyes, allowing the older aunts to wash her body from head to toe. Even washing between her fingers and toes, they cleansed Keun Umma with the utmost respect and care. The aunts, mostly Keun Umma's six daughters, scrubbed the floor where she had urinated and relieved her bowels after passing.

They delicately combed her long gray-white hair, which had never been cut. An elder aunt, Chunji, washed Keun Umma's hands and inserted soaked, uncooked rice in her mouth using a wooden spoon made from a willow tree so that she could have enough food in the after life. Next, she placed one gold coin into Keun Umma's mouth so she would have money to buy a ride on a boat to the afterlife. Subsequently, Chunji added two more gold coins, one in each of Keun Umma's palms, covering them with new gloves made from hemp fiber. Chunji closed her palms forever and placed both folded, wrinkled hands at the center of Keun Umma's chest, tying them together with a hemp rope. The female servants covered her feet with warm hand-made socks and dressed her with new underclothes all made from hemp fiber.

After they finished dressing her, the male servants laid her body on a large, thin "sheet" made of hemp. We used hemp fiber to wrap deceased family members because we believed that it would break down quickly allowing them to return to the earth faster. The female servants then folded the "sheet" in a prescribed way, wrapping Keun Umma like a gift. Following that, the male servants tied hemp rope around her in seven different places, from her neck to her feet to keep her body from moving.

Continuing the burial process, my uncles and cousins gathered bundles of rice straw and tied them together. After the straw was bound, the men brought it to where Keun Umma resided. They placed the bundles of straw in three sections on the floor, then picked Keun Umma's body up, setting her on top of the three bundles. As Keun Umma died during the summer, her body began to decay quickly and the smell was so horrible that my uncles sprinkled soot under her body until she was ready to be buried. The soot absorbed the fluids that dripped from the body and dampened the smell until the funeral began.

Getting ready for the funeral was a long process, and everyone had tasks to perform. The food took days to prepare and all the women and older female children had to observe and participate.

For a funeral in our family, we always made *tteok* (rice cakes). There are several different types of rice cakes, such as *siru-tteok* (pure white rice cake without any coloring), *songpyeon* (half moon shaped cake), *ingeolmi* (soybean powder rice cake), and *mujigae-tteok* (rainbow rice cake). We soaked the uncooked sweet rice overnight until the water was fully absorbed and the rice was ready to cook. After the rice was cooked, we pounded it in a large, carved stone basin. Next, we took the sticky rice and added food coloring made from natural herbs and flowers, and shaped the *tteok*. We also added soybean powder, sesame seeds, red beans, pumpkin seeds, and pine nuts for different texture and tastes.

While the female family members and servants cooked, the male family members and servants were busy making an untreated pine casket. This was to carry Keun Umma to her final resting place in one of the four Yi family mountains in Yesan, Chungcheongnahm-do. The male servants dug the plot for her burial, which was located next to her husband's body, and gathered twigs from the surrounding mountains to cover her entire body during the burial. Once everything was prepared, the family members and the servants all dressed in their white *hanbok*, the traditional Korean clothing for funerals.

The male servants picked up Keun Umma's body and carefully set her on the platform made from trees gathered from the nearby mountain. These men walked slowly toward the mountain carrying the body, and everyone followed. The whole village came together for

Keun Umma's funeral; both the *yangbans* (nobles) and servants paid their respects to Keun Umma since she was related to almost everyone in the village.

The funeral procession trailed up the mountain and once everyone arrived, Keun Umma was taken out of the casket and her hemp-wrapped body placed in the prepared earth. Before the first handful of soil fell on her body, one of the uncles draped red fabric over Keun Umma. The red fabric featured information about Keun Umma: when she was born, when she died, where she was buried, what she accomplished in life, and the names of her six children. After Keun Umma was covered in the fabric, the men of the Yi family laid down the twigs they had collected from around the mountain, placing them horizontally across her until the whole body was covered. After all the twigs were laid down, they placed small stones over the twigs and covered the body with dirt until they had a five-foot-high mound. The mound was then covered with sod, completing the burial process.

After the burial, everyone walked back to the village in Yesan to eat traditionally prepared funeral food.

The *yangban* burial process was only done for the *yangban* families. It was handed down from generation to generation through the elders. My Umma's family in Yesan, Chungcheongnahm-do, continues to do the *yangban* burial process today. The family mountain has been with us for over eight hundred years and elders still teach our family rituals to the younger generations. It is very difficult to lay a person you love to rest, but it helps to do so with the utmost respect and love, which we strive for with the *yangban* burial.

After Umma told me about my family's funeral practices, I was anxious to see what Mr. Kim's family would do for his burial. Umma didn't go to the burial site, which was only about twenty-five meters away from Mr. Kim's home. Umma told me, "Sami, it is not good to see sick or dead people when mothers are pregnant."

However, Appa and I visited the burial site together, and I saw Mr. Kim wrapped in a hemp sheet like Keun Umma. All of his children and his relatives wore a white *hanbok*, except his son, who wore a black uniform with a brimmed hat. He bowed his head when his father's body was lowered into the earth. However, he did not cry like the rest of his family, and I thought that was strange as I felt numb from the whole event. After witnessing the burial, many people in our village returned to Mr. Kim's home and ate in his courtyard, celebrating Harabaji's life.

Chapter 8

Unni

Unni's name is Jin-sun. She is the eldest daughter, born in 1961, the year of the Bull, meaning that Unni was destined for a lifetime of hard work. Tall and skinny with dark brown hair and high cheekbones, Unni is seven years older than me, and during our childhood, she was like a second mother. She had to put her schooling aside at the age of thirteen so that she could help care for her younger siblings.

I love Unni very much, but because of our age difference, I often felt we had little in common. So instead of playing with Unni, I would wonder off by myself to explore the butterflies, grasshoppers, frogs, and wild flowers, especially the white clover. I used the white clover to make rings, necklaces, and bracelets. Sometimes I called the clover *rabbit fur* or *ring flowers*. There were so many flowers, each with its own distinct scent and texture, around the fields, woods, and mountains and I could look at them all day, not seeing the same one twice.

Along the creek, I would cut some twigs and make them into musical instruments called recorders to practice songs. I would also bring home long twigs from black willows, sometimes called pussy willows, for Umma. She would steam them in a big pot, spit into her palms, grab a few strands of the wet, steamed pussy willows, and weave them into baskets used for harvesting. She would also use the bark from the black willows to treat swelling. While I frolicked in the fields with Jin-bok, Unni stayed at home, cooking most of our meals, cleaning, and caring for Jin-hun and Jeong-mi.

During winter, there were many fun activities

to explore. Sometimes, Jin-bok, Jin-hun, and I went sledding on the lakes or frozen rice fields near where we lived. Unni would carry our sled up the mountain because we were too small to carry anything that heavy. At the top of the mountain, we played in the snow making snowmen or throwing snowballs. At home, I ate the icicles off the roof and played *Yut-nori*, a traditional Korean board game played during Lunar New Year. For nourishment, we ate what we had stored during the fall months, and in an effort to keep warm, we consumed lots of spicy food.

Since most of the surface water was frozen, we had to pump our water from the ground well. It was hard work. We did not have any hot water, so Umma boiled the well water for our warm baths. Umma and Unni washed all the clothes and cotton diapers in the freezing river for the whole family using the soap we made during the fall. Every other week, Umma took us to a community bath, the size of a small swimming pool where women and their children bathed in a huge bathtub of steaming water. Winters in Korea were very long, but with so many siblings keeping me busy and entertained, the months passed quickly.

As my parents were farmers, they never had enough money to send us to school. The public school system in Korea was not established when we were children. Only the families with enough money were able to send their children to private schools. Some Korean families sacrificed their eldest child's education so that the younger siblings could go to school, as in the case with Unni. At this time, Appa was already in the U.S. working, so Umma had to rent out a room to a textile manager to supplement our income. However, we were still short each month so when Unni was only thirteen years old, she went to work at a textile manufacturing company in Seongnam Si, Gyeonnggi-do. Unni worked hard without complaint because she wanted to provide education to her younger siblings.

Before we came to America in 1978, Jin-bok had a sponsorship from Canada. A couple paid for Jin-bok to go to school, including her school supplies and uniforms, which helped tremendously with our expense.

At 13 years old, Unni was legally too young to work, so she had to lie about her age to get a job at the textile manufacturing company, and thus made a fake I.D. to show that she was old enough to work. She worked twelve hours a day, seven days a week. Unni wanted to go to school so badly, but she knew she couldn't. Instead, she focused on making sure her younger siblings had enough money to pay for their school tuition each month.

Chapter 9

Fall

Fall was one of my favorite seasons because I got to help Umma gather crops. It was very busy time for our family. Jin-bok and I went to the woods to gather chestnuts, acorns, walnuts, persimmons, *ko-sa-li* (fern), and wild herbs like mugwort, snakeweed (which tastes like spinach when it's steamed), ragwort, mustard, chickweed, and dandelion. We also dug for roots like ginseng, lotus, and ginger, and collected tree bark from the white willow tree before the winter months froze these resources.

One of my favorite things to do during fall was to follow Jin-bok around. She was never afraid of anything, climbing trees far into the woods where we weren't supposed to go. She climbed the chestnut trees and shook them until the nuts fell to the ground, so I could gather the nuts, take the spiky greenish-brown husk off, and give them to Umma to store. We also gathered twigs, pine needles, and pinecones for starting fires.

During the fall, everyone was busy digging sweet potatoes, harvesting rice, wheat, and barley, and gathering all kinds of beans. After gathering everything, we roasted crops, like barley and corn, in order to make tea for the cold winter months. Umma also made tofu and soy sauce from soybeans we harvested from our farm. In addition, she made soap and candles from animal fat, wheat bran, and wheat germ.

Toward the end of fall, Jin-bok and I would go with Umma to gather our Napa cabbages and radishes for *kimchi*. *Kimchi* is a spicy, fermented cabbage dish that is eaten throughout the year and with every meal.

Kimchi took all day to make. First, Umma took the Napa cabbages from our field, peeled off the outer leaves, sliced the cabbages in half, and put them in a large container with sea salt. Umma soaked the cabbages in salty water for four to six hours until they were soggy. In the morning, she drained the salty water, rinsed the cabbages in cold, fresh water from the water pump, and put them aside to let the rest of the water drain from them. Meanwhile, she began chopping vegetables to add to the cabbage. Umma peeled the garlic, smashed it, and put it in a small metal bowl. To add to the smashed garlic, she cut radishes into tiny slices and then added green onions, ginger, and red pepper, mixing them in a large bowl with salt and sugar. Sometimes, she added carrots to the *kimchi*. Finally, Umma took the Napa cabbage halves and stuffed them into the large bowl, one leaf at a time.

Umma put the newly prepared *kimchi* into a large, black clay jar called *hangari*. The jars were buried underground during the winter months for the *kimchi* to ferment, but not freeze. We liked eating fresh *kimchi* better than fermented, so Umma would save some unfermented *kimchi* for us on the side. Sometimes, she would make us *kimchi* soup with old, sour *kimchi* and tofu. It was delicious. For good *kimchi* soup, there has to be just enough sourness and spice. It can get so spicy that your face will get sweaty and red as an apple, leaving your stomach fully satisfied. Most of us couldn't imagine life without *kimchi*.

After making *kimchi*, Umma didn't have time to rest. She would go straight out to the fields to harvest the rice. Most years, she planted two kinds of rice: one short grain, brown rice for eating with *kimchi* and other side dishes, and sweet rice for making cakes. Umma washed the rice for a very long time to get rid of small stones and dirt. It was a long process for Umma to make white rice.

After harvesting, the rice straw was gathered in

bundles and stacked for later use to feed the cow, to make shoes, baskets, ropes, and roofs, and to cover the *kimchi hangari*. Umma also made ropes with rice straw. When you think about it, rice plants are amazing in that they sustained our family, not only feeding us, but also sheltering us and keeping us warm.

Our family made other products from rice, wheat, and barley, such as popped rice and roasted rice for tea. We used wheat or rice to make *makgeolli*, a fermented Korean beer, and soap. To make the soap, Umma would separate the germ and bran from the brown rice and removed the dark side of the germ and bran from the light side. With the outer layer of germ and bran, she would make the soap. Soaking wheat germ and bran in warm water until they were soft enough to make into dough, Umma would put rock bleach in warm water to dissolve and add the bleach to the dough. When Umma added the bleach to the wheat germ, it turned yellowish-brown. She kneaded the mixture until it was firm and then cut the blocks into smaller pieces. She used this soap for washing clothes, but not for our bodies as the soap was too scratchy.

As for *makgeolli*, Umma would take five pounds of soaked wheat and another five pounds of soaked rice, and boil them in fresh cold water with *nuruk* (yeast) until the mixture turned milky white. She then added the hibiscus wildflower called *jin-dal-lai*. The flower gave the *makgeolli* a sour flavor. Jin-bok and I would sneak some *makgeolli* and drink it without letting Umma know. It was so sweet and sour and made us dizzy; it was very fun. To this day, I can still smell and taste *makgeolli* in my mind.

Often Umma made *bo-ri-cha*, a roasted barley tea, for us to drink during the fall and winter months, as a means of keeping us warm and healthy. This tea is incredibly healthy. To this day, if I'm sick with a fever or cannot keep food in my stomach, Umma boils barley to make me this tea. I don't know what compounds are in this barley tea, but if I drink it, I immediately stop vomiting and start to keep food down. *Bo-ri-cha* can help control diarrhea, too. You can drink it hot or cold, but either way, it will lessen the symptoms of illness.

We never visited hospitals when we lived on the farm as we couldn't afford to get sick. Fortunately, we were rarely ill as we were active and ate fresh food every day. We ate the vegetables and wild herbs that grew in the creeks, hills, and mountains near our home.

The earth seemed to know what was best for us.

Chapter 10

The Winter

To prepare for winter, Umma would dig a deep hole in the ground, five or six feet below the surface, to store our food. She covered it with salt and rice straw so the *kimchi*, soybean paste, red pepper paste, roots, grain, and nuts would not freeze during the frigid winter months. We stored chestnuts and sweet potatoes at the top of the hole for easy access when we wanted to roast them.

Sometimes, the winter months in South Korea felt unbearable. The snow was deep and nothing grew. As coal was very expensive, we only used it as a last resort. The only way for my family to keep warm during these freezing winter months was to burn the wood that Jin-bok and I had gathered during the fall. Umma would put the firewood under the handmade brick bedroom floor and the heat from the embers would rise, warming up the room. This method was called the *on-dol* system. An *on-dol* is a fireplace in the kitchen that is built a little lower than the bedrooms so that the heat and smoke spread quickly.

During the winter of 1971, while we were still living in Chungcheong-nahm-do, and Umma was pregnant with my brother, Jin-hun, my family experienced a terrible scare.

One very cold night, Umma used coal to heat the floor as we had run out of wood. However, in the morning, we didn't get up like we usually did. The morning turned into the afternoon, and we were all still asleep. By late afternoon, one of our neighbors, Ajuma, who was also Umma's distant cousin, became concerned and walked over to check up on us. We hadn't been doing our chores like we normally would and it was very unusual for Umma to sleep in late.

Ajuma knocked on our bedroom and called out Umma's name, but there was no answer. Ajuma knew we were still inside the bedroom as our shoes were still lined up outside the door. She waited a few more minutes and called out Umma's name, but again no answer came. Ajuma tried to open the bedroom door, but it was locked from the inside. The door was made from small wooden blocks covered with *hanji* (mulberry paper), so Ajuma decided to poke a hole into one of the wooden blocks to peek inside and was shocked to see the four of us still sleeping on the floor with blankets still covering us.

Ajuma called out to Umma, "Jin-sun's mom, wake-up!"

Again, there was no answer. She began to panic. Thinking something tragic might have happened to us, Ajuma wondered for a moment if Umma had killed her three daughters and committed suicide. Ajuma noticed a faint smell and thought perhaps we had been poisoned by carbon monoxide. She didn't know if it was an accident or an intentional act of Umma's.

Ajuma decided to ask another neighbor to help her get the bedroom door open. They forced open the door and called our names, but still we didn't respond. They tried to shake us awake to no avail, so Ajuma felt for our pulse and noticed that we were still breathing, despite being unconscious. Ajuma carried us outside to get some fresh air, but we still didn't respond. All of the doors and windows were opened to circulate air into our bedroom, but we remained unconscious. Finally, she dragged our bodies to the center of the courtyard near the well and threw cold water on our faces and into our mouths. Thankfully, we all woke up coughing and throwing up. Ajuma asked Umma what had happened to us, but Umma claimed she didn't remember anything.

A few days later, Umma's memory came back, and

she said, "I left the coal on all night because we were so cold. I didn't want the girls to get cold."

Sometime during the night, the flame perished, and the smoke from the coal crept into our bedroom. The carbon monoxide would have killed us if it hadn't been for Ajuma.

After the carbon monoxide poisoning, Umma was very weak for months. She claimed she carried my brother an extra two months in her womb due to her frail nature. As Jin-hun was inside her womb for so long, he was almost ten pounds at birth. My brother was born on July 2, 1970 on the lunar calendar, the year of the Dog.

I never got to thank Ajuma. She passed away even before I heard this story. Umma said that she didn't even know her cousin's name. In those days, you weren't allowed to ask for first names or ages.

There were other activities Umma did during the winter months like knitting blankets, sweaters, hats, socks, scarves, and pants. She learned how to knit from her mother, grandmother, aunts, and great-aunts. There were so many different ways to design sweaters and other items by adding or deleting stitches.

The *yangban* women didn't go outside to work in the fields. Servants did everything for them. The women stayed in their quarters, knitting, weaving, and embroidering. The older women passed on their wisdom on how to be a good wife and good mother to the younger generations during these crafting times.

In December 1975, a neighbor invited me to go to church. It was the only Christian church in our village. I was curious, so I asked for Umma's permission to go. It was a long and cold walk to the church because the snow was so deep. Once I got there, I saw a church bell for the first time in my life. I'd heard the bell ringing on Sundays, but never knew where it came from until that night. It was a small church, and inside I saw a small decorated Christmas tree. It was the most beautiful tree I had ever seen. This experience was only more enriched when I heard the song, "Silent Night," for the first time and fell in love with it. When I came home, I shared everything I had seen and heard with my family, hoping to convey the wonderful experience.

Chapter 11

Ghost Elementary School

On March 1, 1976, when I was eight years old, I went to school for the first time at Shin Kwi Elementary School in Seongnam Si, Gyeonggi-do. Jin-bok and I went to school by ourselves because Umma had three small children to take care of at home. Unni didn't attend school as she had to work and bring in a little extra income to support our family.

Umma knew Jin-bok would take me to school safely since she was going into fourth grade and I was going into first. It took us over an hour to walk to school, but luckily it was a warm day with light winds. Spring was only a few weeks away. It was nice to be out since we had been cooped up all winter long.

The night before school, Umma cut our hair and gave us a warm bath in the courtyard. Since we didn't have running hot water, she boiled cold well water, mixed it with more cold water, and gave each of us a clean bath. She rubbed our underarms and necks and washed our hair with homemade dark-brown soap. When Umma threw the water gently against my cold skin to rinse off the soap, it felt warm in the cold winter night. Unfortunately, Umma had to give us quick baths since it was icy cold at night.

After the bath, she dried us with small towels and sent us into the bedroom where all eight of us slept. The room was crowded with thick, colorful blankets handmade by Umma and Weh-Halmoni (Umma's mother). The bedroom was very warm because Umma used the *on-dol* system. Our floor felt about eighty degrees, a stark contrast from the frigid outside air.

Umma clipped our fingernails and toenails and

cleaned our ears with an ear cleaner that was made from a bamboo stick. All of the children then went to sleep while Umma stayed up late into the night drying our clothes. She and Unni had washed them earlier in the river. After the clothes were dried, she ironed them and laid them out along with her hand knitted socks for us to wear the next morning.

After everything was set out, she carried a *yo-gang* (chamber pot) outside in the snow to empty near the front gate. The urine melted the snow quickly. However, our feces were saved for later use in fertilizing vegetables on our farm. It smelled really horrible, especially when we had to wait a few days before it was dumped in the field.

After she got back into the bedroom, she lay next to Jin-suk and Jeong-mi and drifted off to sleep. The next day, Umma was the first to get up and put more wood into the *on-dol* to keep the bedroom warm. Umma got up early in the mornings even during the winter months. That day, she arose at four o'clock to make sure we woke up early enough to get dressed, eat breakfast, and go to school on time.

The sun was out and the air was chilly, but as we walked to school, we got warmer by the minute. I was so excited that I didn't realize how cold it was or how far we had to walk since our school was three miles away. On our way, I marveled at so many beautiful things, like the pine trees, still green as ever, and wild flowers popping up from the earth beside the unpaved road, yet muddy from the melting snow. The flowers were purple, yellow, and white and encompassed the land, moving against the wind. They looked as though they were dancing with joy and reaching toward the heavens.

In Korea, during the 1970s, families did not send their children to pre-school or kindergarten as those classes didn't exist. The children in Korea were much older than the children in the United States when they entered first grade. Most of my classmates were eight years old.

I had to attend school for nine hours a day, from eight in the morning until about five o' clock in the afternoon, six days a week, Monday through Saturday. On Saturdays, school lasted from eight until about noon. At school, we learned how to count in Arabic, Sino-Korean, and Pure-Korean.

After learning how to count, I had to learn *hangul*, the Korean language. *Hangul* has fourteen basic consonants and ten basic vowels. From the basic twenty-four characters, you form words. To do that, you always need at least one consonant and one vowel to form a meaningful word.

Whenever I had a question, I stood next to my wooden desk and raised my right hand until I was given permission to speak by my teacher. After I finished asking my question, I had to remain standing until the teacher allowed me to be seated. We had to have respect for our teachers at all times. If we didn't listen, he or she would take a ruler, tell us to open our hands, and slap us until our hands turned raw and red. I didn't want to bring shame upon my parents, so I always behaved.

If we were late to school, we had to hold our chairs in the air for however many minutes we were late. It was painful. My arms felt like they were going to fall off. The teachers also slapped the ruler on the hands of students who didn't cut their fingernails short. I was hit several times. I never forgot about it because it burned so terribly.

In addition to studying, we also had to do chores around the school. We swept and waxed the wooden floors in our classroom and corridors once a week. The children were asked to pick up trash around the school and to sweep the school grounds as well.

The boys sat on one side of the classroom while the girls sat on the other side. In the center of the classroom, there was a stove that kept the room warm during the winter. The bathrooms were outside, and I did not like going there because I was told by other students that a ghost was there to catch whoever ventured into there. Even the name of our school, Shin Kwi Elementary, can mean ghost when the words are swapped and read as *kwi-shin*. Every time I had to go to the bathroom, I thought I might see a ghost, and whenever I opened the bathroom door, my heart pounded with fear. The bathrooms never had lights, which made them appear even more ominous. The fear never went away as long as I attended Shin Kwi Elementary School.

After attending Shin Kwi for a while, all the excitement I had at the start of school ceased. I did not like going to school because Jin-bok and I had to walk three miles each way. We had to do it six times a week. It felt like being in the ocean without ever seeing land. The winter months were the worst because the snow was deep and cold. Jin-bok and I only had knitted socks, scarves, gloves, and pants that our Umma made for us. None of them were waterproof, thus they got wet and cold very quickly. Later, when our brother Jin-hun was old enough to go to school, Jin-bok gave him a piggyback ride so he would not get too tired or too cold. Jin-bok did these things for me too. She always pretended to be strong and tough, and often felt like she needed to protect her younger siblings.

When Jin-bok and I walked back from school, we would sometimes go through the woods and pick wild pears and flowers to eat. We pretended that the North Koreans were hiding in the woods, waiting to kidnap us and take us back to North Korea. That was pretty scary for me, and I had nightmares from what I heard from other children and adults in town about people that had disappeared for no reason. Many believed North Koreans came at night to kidnap South Koreans and take them back across the border. Mountains and endless pine trees surrounded our home, and if North Koreans wanted to kidnap us, they would have had plenty of opportunities.

Often, Jin-bok and I went up to the mountains to pick wild flowers before we got home from school. We ate the aromatic pink wildflowers called *jin-dal-lai*, savoring their sour taste. Umma told us to pick the flowers and bring them back home, so that she could use them as flavoring for Korean beer.

A Chicken for Dinner

Our farm in Seongnam-si was humble. My family had a few chickens that we raised for eggs and meat, and a single cow we borrowed from Halmoni to collect milk and to plow our fields. We also kept two dogs to keep watch over the farm.

Umma got up early to feed the chickens dried corn and worms every morning. When we had a special guest over, one of us would kill a chicken for dinner. The chickens seemed to know when we were going to kill one of them and they made a lot of noise, running all over the cage screaming, their feathers fanning up and down. Umma didn't like to kill chickens. She never got used to it. It was painful for her to watch or perform the slaughter.

I saw Umma kill a chicken once when I was about seven years old. Umma cut the chicken's neck quickly. It was over in an instant. I doubt the chicken felt any pain. After she removed the chicken's head, she put the body inside a pot of hot boiling water for few seconds before plucking the feathers. I will never forget the way it looked as she plucked its feathers–like pulling weeds from a moist soil. I don't remember being frightened; I just felt strange and numb.

When the chicken was cooked, it made for a tasty meal. I have never tasted chicken like that anywhere else. It is difficult for me to describe the aroma, flavor, or texture in English. The meat was tender and smooth, and the smell was so delicious. It was flavored with chestnuts, garlic, ginseng, rice, jujube fruit, black pepper, salt, and green onions. Despite the incredible taste, I would never want to kill a chicken unless it was necessary to feed my family.

I still don't like to eat meat very much, perhaps because I watched that chicken's head being cut from its body. Red meat is an even bigger turn off because I can still smell the blood from the cow when it was slaughtered. I eat fruits and vegetables if I have a choice. I don't enjoy preparing meat though I will eat it if someone serves it to me.

Eating chicken or other meat on the farm wasn't a pleasant experience for me as preparing them was a lot of work. It was gruesome to watch animals being killed so that we could eat, but I will always cherish those childhood memories.

Chapter 13

A Package from America

In 1958, Komo, Appa's older sister, sent us a package in a light brown box. We had never received a package from anyone before. Filled with excitement, we yearned to discover what was inside as Komo had been living in America for about 12 years. We jumped up and down in the small, one bedroom home that all eight of us shared as Umma opened the box with her kitchen knife. It was the same knife she used for cutting everything from vegetables to thread to the umbilical cords of her children. The box had a strange yellow wrapping on it. I later discovered it was tape, but at the time, I'd never seen tape before.

Umma didn't know how to describe what was inside the box. It was filled with jars, but none of us knew what was in the jars. We could not read the labels and the items looked strange. The jar with the red substance had some black seeds in it. She'd sent us one jar of strawberry jam and one jar of peanut butter. In spite of their strange appearance, I wanted to taste the jars' contents. I didn't know what to expect, wondering if it would be sweet or bitter. I put one spoonful of peanut butter and one spoonful of strawberry jam into my mouth, and tasted them separately. I was so surprised at how different they were. The strawberry jam was the sweetest and yummiest thing I had ever tasted, while the peanut butter was creamy and rich. It was hard to swallow, but it left my mouth with a flavor and aroma I will never forget. I did not spread them over bread. As a matter of fact, I never saw bread until I came to America. My siblings and I ate all the strawberry jam and peanut butter that day. I felt so special that I had a Komo in America.

Komo married an African American G.I. named Robert, whom she met when he was stationed in South Korea in the 1950s. They had a little girl named Susie, who was born in Korea in 1958. When Susie was six weeks old, they moved to the United States. It was a difficult time for Komo. She left her home for the first time to live in a country she knew very little about, hoping that life would be better in America. She was in for a big surprise.

Komo thought she could work and make a lot of money to send back to South Korea where her mother, brothers, and sister were living. Life in Korea was a mess after the Korean War, and Komo thought nothing could be worse than that, but she was wrong. Although America was at peace and she could easily buy food, she struggled with racial segregation as she was involved in an interracial relationship. Komo didn't know what segregation meant until she came to America.

When she was in South Korea, white or black men were the same. They were both risking their lives, protecting the South Koreans from the North Koreans. The white and black Americans ate and slept the same. They both liked to drink and smoke, and they both liked Korean women. Upon moving to America, she began to see differences in the way some of her Korean girlfriends who had married white GI's were treated in California as compared to her treatment. She couldn't have anticipated these racial differences. Even in Korea, Komo's original birth certificate is marked "X" for marrying a non-Korean. When you have an "X" on your birth certificate, it means you are deceased. My great uncle, Jeong, felt that Komo was already dead for marrying a non-Korean, but even more so for marrying a black man. Sometime during the 1960s, he went to the recording office and put an "X" on top of her name. Appa and I didn't discover this information until April 4, 2007 when Appa and I made a trip to Korea.

Komo's husband had never told her about the racial discrimination in America. Even if he had, she wouldn't have understood. She barely understood what her husband was saying. They communicated in simple language with hand gestures.

She couldn't even tell her family in Korea what was happening as she didn't want to worry them as her family wasn't doing so well in Korea. Most Korean cities were in ruins, especially near Seoul, and there were so many hungry people. In the 1950s and early 1960s, South Koreans in rural areas only had one meal a day, a simple bowl of *jook* (rice porridge). She internalized all her feelings, frustrations, and struggles.

After the war, Korea was divided into two nations: North Korea and South Korea. North Korea was a communist nation aided by the Soviet Union and China, while South Korea was aided by the United States and the United Nations. After the Korean War, the United States kept sending troops to South Korea because the tensions between North and South had not been resolved. Komo's husband, Robert, was sent to South Korea as a U.S. soldier during this period, leading to him and Komo meeting.

In the early 1970s, Komo and Robert divorced. I don't know why, but Umma told me it was because Uncle Robert didn't want to sponsor our family. I'm sure it was more than that, but back then I was a child, and children didn't ask questions. Komo soon married a man named Bert. He was also an American G.I. and was willing to sponsor my family in South Korea. Komo told Appa that education was free in America, and that if a man worked hard enough, his children could have anything they wanted. Appa wanted to make our lives better, but he was scared to go to another country to try to make a living, feed his children, and educate them in English. However, he felt that he had no other choice but to leave Korea. Appa left for America in November 1977, leaving his wife and six children behind in Korea until he had enough money to send for us. He hoped his move would provide new opportunities and prosperity, enabling him to start his life over. Komo was able to sponsor Appa to come to America, but she didn't have enough money for all of us. Everyone in our village thought that Appa wasn't coming back for his family. Fortunately, they were wrong.

After arriving in America, Appa quickly found a job at Oki Nursery in Sacramento, California. After six months, he repaid his brother-in-law Bert all the money he had borrowed to come to America, plus interest. He sent the rest of his money to South Korea so that Umma could buy us all plane tickets to Sacramento.

My family and I were very excited and hopeful. I thought America was going to be like heaven. I'd heard from friends and their parents that in America streets were made of gold, and I would be able to meet movie stars. So many of our family friends and relatives wished they could go to America as well. I felt sorry for them and I didn't know why we were able to go to America while others couldn't.

It was such a bittersweet time. My siblings and I were ecstatic for the move. My parents didn't need to pay for our school tuition anymore, and my oldest sister, Unni, didn't have to work to pay for our education either. She could attend public school and get an education for herself. Unni was so happy to attend school because she'd been working twelve hours a day, seven days a week at a textile factory. I was particularly excited to make new friends in a strange new country.

It was also a sad time as we had to say good-bye to our relatives, friends, and neighbors we'd known since childhood. My family gave away many of our belongings. Umma had a hard time making decisions about what to give away, but we could only take what we could carry onto the airplane and some boxes and suitcases that went in the baggage area. Umma trusted that God would take care of her and her children in this next chapter of our lives.

Chapter 14

Komo

Komo lived through a difficult childhood in South Korea. She was the second of five children and her father, my Harabaji, passed away when she was eleven years old. Soon after that, my Halmoni, Soo-jae Kim, married Sauk-Myeong Song. Halmoni was forced to remarry quickly because food was scarce during the 1940s, making it nearly impossible to survive without a husband to support you. As a result, Halmoni married the first person who was willing to feed her children.

This created tremendous anxiety for Komo and Appa, who were still very young at the time. Komo was eleven and my Appa was seven. They knew that living with a new father could be difficult. He was not a cruel stepfather, but they knew he would not love them like their own biological father. They knew he would not think of their education or welfare before his own children.

Halmoni had a son with her new husband. She had several more children with him, yet they all died very young, leaving only one survivor. Halmoni began to ignore her other children from her first marriage, feeding the table scraps to them and treating Komo and Appa like her house servants.

Appa did not have much to his name. Clothing was difficult to come by, and Umma once told me that Appa didn't have a single new pair of underwear when he married her. Also, Halmoni forced Appa to do chores from sunup to sundown, and thus, he sometimes felt like he was a slave.

Komo decided to leave her home early. She thought that if she left, there would be one less mouth to feed. During this time, Komo married an older Korean man named Mr. Kim. They had a son together, Ho-kyeong Kim. On the other hand, Appa kept busy by working hard for his stepfather. He did everything he could to please his stepfather, constantly trying to prove his worth.

Appa told me that his sister, Komo, was a beautiful woman. She had fair skin, long, light-brown hair, and beautiful eyes, always capturing male attention.

When she married her first husband, times were very difficult. After the war, many people didn't have jobs or a place in which to live. Most people were very poor. Komo's first husband couldn't find work to feed his mother, his wife, and their young son, so Komo decided to leave them and start a new life with Robert, an American G.I. who wanted to marry her. It is possible that Komo never told her new husband that she was already married. She thought perhaps one day she could come back for her son, but she never did. Her first husband was heartbroken when she left him and didn't live long after Komo left. No one knows if he committed suicide or if he died from a broken heart.

Komo never went back to Korea for her first son after she married Robert and became pregnant with her second child. Some of our relatives remember seeing her first son and her mother-in-law in the street, holding bowls and begging for food. Komo must have felt there was nothing else she could have done at that time.

The night before Komo decided to leave her young son, Ho-kyeong, and her husband, she cried all night. She felt like she didn't have another choice.

Komo left for the United States to begin a new life, but she never forgot her siblings or Ho-kyeong. She sent money to her young sister and to her mother to help take care of Ho-kyeong, but they never gave the money to him.

Twenty-five years later, when Komo finally visited her son, now a married man, he told her he'd never received any money. Komo's daughter-in-law didn't want to meet her, ignoring Komo's explanation for her absence and proclaiming, "How can I meet someone who leaves her young son without ever coming back?"

The daughter-in-law just couldn't believe that Halmoni, Komo's mother, and Bong-mo, Komo's sister, had spent all of the money intended for Ho-kyeong.

Chapter 15

Leaving for America

May 2, 1978 is a day forever ingrained in my memory. On this day, my family and I left our home, our village, and our country. The place of my childhood would now be traded for an adventure into the unknown. Umma only had room to pack clothes, blankets, and a few dishes that she'd received from her mother as a wedding gift. It was a difficult time for Umma. This uprooting left her feeling bereft, and she cried while packing.

Umma felt Appa was too impatient to be a farmer. A farmer had to be patient, as he had to wait until his crops matured fully before harvesting. Umma claimed,

"You can only plant the seed, water, and watch your crops grow. The rest is up to God. God will bring rain to cover the ground and nourish the earth. You just need to weed sometimes and wait."

However, Appa struggled with Umma's advice. His ambition made him impatient, so he decided to start a trucking company. However, this new career path ended up killing a little boy. I don't know the boy's name, and I dare not to ask Appa. For many years, I thought it was only a dream, but it really happened. In some ways, I am glad that I don't know the details. It was such a sad incident. Appa had to sell almost everything and give it to the boy's family. Appa felt like he no longer had any reason to stay in South Korea. He was frustrated, and nothing seemed to go his way. This tragic event led to our immigration to America.

I think part of Appa's problem was that he never discussed business ideas or plans with Umma. Appa never included Umma in any of his decisions. This is also an aspect of Korean culture. Men do not discuss their business plans with their wives. Traditionally, women were to stay out of men's business; however, if these business plans affected the whole family, family communication was necessary. Communication, at the very least, is necessary with your wife to keep peace and trust within the family. Umma always seemed to have more common sense than Appa. He claimed Umma, like most women, talked way too much. He told her to stay quiet, but Umma never listened, ignoring him and driving Appa crazy. Appa is a very quiet man, hardly ever speaking, rarely smiling, and always seemingly upset about something. I was always afraid to speak to him. I was never to interrupt him when he spoke; if I did, he would smack my mouth.

After packing and loading the boxes and suitcases, it was time to say our good-byes to friends and neighbors. I had two friends, Jin-suk Ko and another girl. I can't remember her first name, just her face.

However, she had the same last name as Umma. Her father's name was Bok-man Yi. Her parents and my parents were very close.

When I told my girlfriends that I was moving to America, they said, "Sami, you are so lucky. You get to see movie stars, such as *Wonder Woman* and *Bionic Man*, on the streets in America." Wonder Woman and Bionic Man were two popular TV characters in the 1970s and early 1980s. I was so sad to be leaving and scared that I had to ride on an airplane to get there that I didn't care if I was going to see the movie stars or not.

After we hugged our friends and neighbors farewell, our family drove to the Kimpo International Airport in Seoul. It was a long taxi ride to the airport because of the traffic, but along the way I got to see tall buildings for the first time in my life. I had never seen so many cars and people. My parents had never taken my siblings and me outside our village because we couldn't afford it. There were too many of us. Only

Appa had traveled outside our village while visiting relatives or looking for work in the city, so that taxi ride was my first experience in the world outside of Seongnam-si.

On our way to the airport, we stopped to visit one of Appa's cousins, Kwang-mo Jeong, who owned a Korean restaurant and happened to live not too far from the airport. She ran the restaurant with her husband, Hwang, and their three children. They made us *ja-jang mein*, black noodles with vegetables. It had pork, onions, potatoes, squash, carrots, and a lot of garlic. They made the noodles fresh by hand from wheat flour and then cut them with thin ceramic plates. The sauce was black from black beans. I still remember how it tasted. It was so delectable, but we all had to wash our mouths because the sauce made our mouths black.

When we arrived at the airport, my Sahm-chohn (maternal uncle), Chan-ku, was waiting. He'd come up all the way from Busan to say good-bye to our family.

When it was time to get on the airplane, our Sahm-chohn was so sad that we were leaving Korea. He thought he would never see us again. He and Umma cried together. Weh-Halmoni had died when Sahm-chohn was just an infant, so he thought of Umma as his second mother. Umma was concerned that she may not see her brothers and sisters again. As the second oldest of nine siblings, she felt responsible for them.

When it was time to say good-bye to Sahm-chohn, he hugged each of us. Warm tears slowly ran down from his cheeks to his throat. I could see him trying to hold back his tears in front of Umma because Korean men aren't supposed to cry in public.

For me, one of the most exciting moments in my life was when I saw the airplane for the first time. The airplane on which my family and I flew to America was a big 747. It was like a huge bird. I had never seen such a contraption. I didn't know what Umma was thinking or what was on her mind because I was consumed with the airplane. She was still so young. She was only thirty-six, but having so many children made her feel and look older than she was. Once we all got on the plane, we sat in our seats and waited for the plane to take off. We couldn't see through the windows because we all sat in center seats as they were the cheapest seats. When our plane was ready to take off, I could hear the loud noise coming from the sides, making the backend shake so hard. I was so nervous and frightened that I grabbed Umma's right hand very tightly and closed my eyes.

Part II

America

Dreaming in English
A Memoir

Chapter 16

The First Night

My family arrived at the San Francisco International Airport on May 2, 1978 when I was 10 years old. It was already dark, but from the air, the city looked beautiful with so many lights. There were tall buildings of many different shapes and sizes and the Golden Gate Bridge looked golden in the night sky. Soon after the bridge disappeared, we landed. I felt dizzy and nervous as though I was still in the air. I didn't know what to do or where to go, so I followed Umma and Unni.

Five hours earlier, we had landed on Oahu in Hawaii. However, I thought we had arrived in California

because we had flown for over seven hours. I didn't
own a watch, but I knew we'd been in the air for a long
time. I couldn't wait to stand and walk around, but
there were too many people inside the airplane and we
were crowded in our small seats. Most passengers on
the plane were Koreans. I thought because we all had
black hair, if one of us were to get lost, it would be very
difficult to find each other. Unfortunately, that was
precisely what happened to me during the layover at the
Honolulu Airport.

I wanted to wash my hands when I got back onto
the plane, but instead, I sat in the first seat I saw in the
aisle and waited until my family passed me to find their
seats. I thought they were going to sit next to me, but
they sat in the far back of the plane. I got up and used
the restroom and sat back in my seat, searching for my
family to no avail. Instead of asking for help, I got up
to look for them, but the stewardess asked me to sit
down and to put on my seat belt. I sat there waiting for

the plane to take off; however, instead of taking off, the flight attendants announced they were looking for a child. I didn't know at the time that Umma was looking for me, so I just sat there until I saw Umma pass me.

Upon finding me, Umma said with a concerned look, "Sami, why are you sitting here by yourself? You were supposed to follow me so that we could all sit together."

She grabbed my hand and pulled me toward the back of the plane where the rest of my family were sitting. The plane had been delayed for twenty minutes because of me.

When we were in the Honolulu Airport, Umma explained that during the layover, we'd have our health inspected and get our green cards and social security cards. In those days, all the green cards and social security cards were issued at the Honolulu Airport for the Koreans. Umma was very tired as she hadn't had much sleep. She needed to get her children off the airplane and through the health inspection, but she didn't speak one word of English and quickly became overwhelmed. Appa was there to help at the San Francisco Airport, but that didn't help Umma in Honolulu.

After Umma got us off the plane, she didn't know where to turn, making her confused and scared. Standing with her head held high, she took a long breath and told us to follow her. Even though she didn't speak English, she tried to use her body language to communicate with the airport workers. Unfortunately, no one seemed to understand. The airport workers weren't rude; in fact, they wanted to help her. However, they just couldn't understand what she was saying. Finally, someone approached Umma to help. It seemed strange at first because we didn't expect a dark skinned woman that looked like a Native Hawaiian to speak to us in Korean. She had frizzy, short black hair and dark brown skin. She wore a blue uniform. To this day,

I'm not sure if she worked at the airport because we never saw her after she helped us in Honolulu. This kind woman directed us to the right office to get our paperwork completed before we left for California. As we were wearing long-sleeved shirts and jackets, I remember walking outside the airport to go to another building and feeling extremely hot and uncomfortable. I'd worn my pink nylon blouse and a blue polyester skirt as they were my best clothes. This was the uniform I'd worn to school in Korea. Unfortunately, the polyester fabric didn't breathe well, so I was sweating profusely in the warm Hawaiian climate.

The kind lady told Umma to take us to the nearby restroom and change our clothes into something lighter and shorter. It was a relief to dress in something cooler. While in the restroom, I realized that I had to use the toilet. As it was the first time I used a flushing toilet, I was scared to sit on it at first. Finally, the urge to go was so overwhelming that I pulled down my underwear and sat down. I was scared that if I flushed the toilet, I would fall down and be flushed into the unknown. I cried and wouldn't get off the seat, but the kind dark skinned lady helped me use it and stayed in the stall until I finished and flushed the toilet. After we changed, the lady took us inside a white building and we had our photos taken for green cards. Before going into another building to get our health checked, we all needed immunizations. Getting shots was so painful, and I remember hiding under the table, crying and not wanting to come out. Unlike me, my sister, Jeong-mi, took the shots bravely. I still remember those shots; they were scarier than flying on an airplane.

As I walked to the next plane, I saw my first palm trees. I'd been so uncomfortably warm that I hadn't noticed all the beautiful trees and the bright blue sky until I was going back to the main building of the airport.

On the flight to San Francisco, I remember feeling

trapped and nauseated, causing me to throw up all over myself. The stewardess felt sorry for me, so she gave me a plastic toy plane to occupy myself. When I was able to look out of the small window of the plane, the clouds looked like a bunch of cotton balls stuck together or like fresh snow in the morning. From the air, I wanted to jump down and play on the clouds as if it was the first snow of winter back home. When I looked beyond the clouds, I could see the hazy line that divided heaven and earth.

As we approached San Francisco Airport, I could see dark areas from above. The plane got lower and lower and my ears plugged. It was painful, but I was so excited that I would be seeing Appa and America that I didn't let it bother me. As we got closer to the ground, I was able to see brown hills and dark, green trees. I soon saw a massive dark green body of water that I later found out was the other side of the Pacific Ocean.

When we made it to the waiting area, Appa and

Komobo, my American uncle, were there to greet us. We hadn't seen Appa for six months and it was Jin-suk, only two years old, who first recognized and ran to him, calling out "Appa." It was a wonderful reunion and Appa looked so happy to see us. We all hugged, cried, and laughed; I was so excited to see Appa that I didn't even notice Komobo until we all walked up to pick up our suitcases. This huge man with brown curly hair and a red face helped us with our bags, speaking to us in English although no one knew what he was saying. He didn't really smile, but he wanted to help us and Appa seemed very comfortable with him. Appa introduced us all, and even though Komobo knew our names, he didn't pronounce them correctly, but it was close enough. After we gathered our belongings, we went to the parking lot where two cars awaited our departure. After every suitcase and box was packed, we left the airport and headed east toward Rancho Cordova. By then, it was very dark. The night was clear and the air felt clean and fresh. I remember Komobo's car was white and had four doors with a huge trunk that could accommodate most of our suitcases. I had never seen such a huge car, and I was really excited to ride in it. We didn't have to wear seatbelts back then, so the young ones, like Jin-suk and Jeong-mi, sat on Umma's and Unni's laps.

It was a beautiful drive to Rancho Cordova. I remember sitting in the back of the car and thinking how nice it felt to have my two feet on the ground after so many hours in the air. No one slept during the car ride because everyone wanted to see what America looked like. It took about two hours to get to Rancho Cordova where our Komo lived. I remember looking out of the window of the car while we were still driving and thinking, "Am I in heaven or on earth?" There were white lights in the front of the car, which twinkled in the dark night, and when I looked to my right, I saw many red lights facing the opposite direction, only enhancing my awe. The lane on the freeway was very wide, and some parts of it were dark. I couldn't see what was outside of the car, but the visible stars in the night sky looked smaller than I remembered in Korea.

When we finally arrived at Komo's house late at night, all four of our American cousins, Susie, Robert, William, and Dennis, were waiting for us. Meeting my cousins in America was a remarkable time for me and it was comforting to know that we had a family in America since this was to be our new home. However, it felt odd to be lying on the floor in a new country when just twelve hours previously I'd been in South Korea with my family, speaking Korean. Now, I needed to learn a new language.

We stayed up late talking with my cousins. Komo translated for us before she had to go to sleep. My family and I slept on the floor of Komo's living room, and my first night in America proved to be very long and tiring. There were so many noises around the house. The sounds of the clock, washer, dryer, and refrigerator kept me up all night. I had never seen a refrigerator before, and I was amazed by something that kept food cold for many hours, if not days. Komo even was able to keep some of the food cold for months. In Korea, we didn't have a refrigerator. We'd eaten fresh food everyday from spring through fall, and in winter, we'd buried our food underground so that it wouldn't freeze.

The next day, my family and Komo's family threw me a very small birthday party, and we had *ttolk gouk* soup. It was my very first birthday party even though I was ten years old. In Korea, everyone turned one year older on the first day of the Lunar New Year. On this day, almost every family in Korea makes *ttolk gouk*, a rice soup.

Ttolk gouk is made from rice that has been soaked and pounded into sticky dough. The dough is rolled into a long, skinny tube, then sliced into small, thin pieces about one-eighth of an inch thick. You put the pieces into a pot that is boiling with either fish or beef broth, then you add eggs, carrots, green onions, black pepper, garlic, and *mandu* (pot stickers) to the soup.

After eating the soup, you become one year older. It generally doesn't matter if you were born on January first or December thirty-first.

There are two occasions when Koreans celebrate their birthdays: the one-hundredth day of life and the sixty-first birthday based on the lunar calendar. Many Koreans celebrate the one-hundredth day after birth because previously many children did not survive past their one-hundredth day. Also, Koreans celebrate the sixty-first birthday because, in the past, many elders died before they turned sixty-one.

Having *ttolk gouk* soup on that birthday was a very special day for me even though it wasn't New Year's Day. It marked a new beginning in America, and I will always remember it.

Chapter 17

Our First Home

The day after my first birthday party, we packed our belongings and headed to Sacramento. Komo and Komobo drove us to our new home, a place called the Rosewood Apartments. We were given apartment number 30, which had one bedroom and one bathroom. It was where Appa had been living by himself for the past six months.

It was a shock to see so many apartments stuck together with so many people living in one place. The buildings looked old and plain. There were some trees and bushes, but there were no mountains, hills, rivers, creeks, or the smells of flowers that we were used to.

At first, I felt caged inside an endless dream. I closed my eyes to see if the view was just a dream, but when I opened my eyes, I was still standing just outside the car with the old, beige building looming over me.

All eight of us lived in that one bedroom apartment for two years until the manager discovered us. The manager decided it wasn't safe, so our family moved to a three-room apartment with two bathrooms.

We had no open spaces to grow food and to run around. Umma was very sad, and I quickly found out that America was not heaven at all. We did not see movie stars on the streets; all I saw was Appa and Umma working long hours at the Oki Nursery and Unni, who was nearly seventeen years old, having to watch all five of us like she had done back in Korea.

When I arrived in Sacramento in May 1978, I couldn't begin school because the summer vacation was just around the corner. Appa and Umma decided to keep us home until fall, so I had nothing to do. The weather was starting to get warm and I didn't want to stay cooped up inside for very long. When I finally ventured outside our apartment, I made many new friends in our complex as the apartments had many Korean immigrants living there, so it was easy to meet other Korean kids. Having new friends who spoke the same language was helpful, and I didn't think about Korea as often.

One day, Unni was talking to a new friend, Hae-kyeong Lee, and not paying close attention to us when a drunk driver hit Jin-suk. There was an old English walnut tree across the street where we lived and Jin-suk liked to cross the street to pick up walnuts and bring them back to play with them. She kept going back and forth for a while because there weren't any cars. Unni kept an eye on her, but when she turned her head to talk with Hae-kyeong for a few seconds, the drunk driver drove by really fast and hit Jin-suk, taking off toward Kiefer Boulevard. I don't even think the driver knew he hit a child. Luckily, there was a witness who called an ambulance and a police officer. The ambulance took Jin-suk to the University of California, Davis Medical Center in Sacramento, where she was treated and released in the evening. I remember Jin-suk coming home with a pink baby blanket and with one black shoe. She lost her other shoe when the driver hit her. Fortunately, Jin-suk wasn't seriously injured, just bruised a little. All she asked for was her other black shoe. We all hugged and kissed Jin-suk. A few weeks later in the mail, Umma and Appa received an ambulance bill for $150.

Unni had much more responsibility compared to her American friends of the same age. Life in America wasn't much easier than life in Korea for Unni as only the language and location changed.

Our first summer in America ended as September rolled around and it was time for us to attend public school in Sacramento. It was an exciting time, and I couldn't wait to learn English and make new friends, but I didn't know what my classmates would look like or what they would think of me. School started at the beginning of September after Labor Day. Komo drove Umma, Appa, Jin-hun, Jeong-mi, and me to James W. Marshall Elementary School in Rosemont. I wore a long sleeved pink blouse and a pleated navy skirt that I'd brought from South Korea. It was small, but it was the only outfit that looked decent enough to wear to school. Once on campus, the school secretary put Jeong-mi into kindergarten, Jin-hun into first grade, and me into fourth grade.

Unni and Jin-bok went to different schools. Unni went into the ninth grade at Hiram Johnson High School. She was seventeen years old, but she was not allowed to graduate until she finished all four years of high school, especially since she had no records stating that she'd attended middle school.

Jin-bok was placed into seventh grade at Albert

Einstein Middle School. At the time, the school did not offer English as a second language, so she had to teach herself how to read and write as Appa and Umma couldn't afford a tutor. Fortunately, she learned to speak English quickly, but struggled with reading and writing.

Jin-bok was at an age where she wanted to do as she pleased and didn't care to listen to anyone else. She made friends very quickly and got into trouble just as fast. She had a hard time adjusting to American life, and since she was so eager to fit in, she started using drugs and drinking. I don't know how she obtained the drugs or alcohol, but I found some in her closet one afternoon.

I had been playing hide-and-seek with Jin-hun and Jeong-mi when I stumbled across the contraband. I didn't know what I had found in Jin-bok's closet, so I showed them to Umma. She didn't know what drugs were either. When Jin-bok came home, Umma asked her what they were and where she got them. Jin-bok didn't even open her mouth. When Appa asked her the same question, she didn't answer. He was so upset and frustrated that he spanked her, but still she wouldn't say anything. Appa sent Jin-bok to her room and told her not to come out until she told him where she got the drugs and beer, but she never told him. Appa and Umma never went to her school to find out because they didn't speak English. They'd never had these problems back in Korea, and as a result, felt ashamed.

I remember my parents fighting over their move to America. Had it really provided them with a better life? After the drug incident, Appa was never the optimistic person he'd been before and stopped attending the adult school where he'd been improving his English skills.

Had Appa learned English, perhaps he would have found a better-paying job. Perhaps he could have bought us new clothes and new shoes. Jin-bok never forgave me for telling Umma about the drugs. I'd never meant to cause her any trouble, but she still didn't trust me with another secret for a long time.

Chapter 18

Mint Chocolate Chip Ice Cream

The summer of 1978 was our first summer in America and by that time, we'd lived in Sacramento for only a few months. Our complex was a crowded place with apartments so close to each other, I was able to hear neighbors yelling and their toilets flushing. There were a lot of older folks, children, and especially several new immigrants from Korea seeing as 1978 was the peak year for Korean immigration.

A large number of Koreans immigrated to the United States in the 1980s. In South Korea, most Koreans were struggling. The median income rose from eighty dollars per year in 1961 to one thousand dollars in the 1980s, but that was scarcely enough to survive. Many South Koreans settled in New York, Washington, D.C., or California. Those in California settled in Los Angeles, San Francisco, and Sacramento. Many worked jobs that Americans didn't want to do, like cleaning office buildings, washing people's clothes, tending to the fields, and working in restaurants. Still, many Koreans couldn't find jobs because of the language barrier. To combat this unemployment, some Koreans decided to open their own businesses: grocery stores, gas stations, restaurants, dry cleaners, shoe repair shops, beauty salons, hotels, car dealerships, gift shops, bookstores, and shopping centers.

During the summer of 1978, there wasn't much to do in our crowded apartment since school hadn't yet begun. It was difficult to stay indoors when the weather outside was so warm and the sky so blue. My sisters and I stayed near our apartment building, playing hide and seek and looking for other children. We saw many children, but Umma wouldn't let us wander off on our own, thus it was difficult for us to make new friends.

The only thing we did, other than playing in front of our apartment building, was ride in Appa's green car that I coined the "Green Tank." It was so large that all eight of us could fit inside at the same time. One Sunday morning, Appa told us that we were going to our first church outing. I was a little surprised as Appa had neither attended church in Korea nor had he ever shown any interest in Christianity. However, Appa had been to this church in Sacramento several times since the previous November and knew many Koreans at the church. I was very nervous, but tried not to let Appa know it.

Appa never locked the Green Tank. It was old, the seats were worn and torn, and the radio didn't work. Back then, we didn't wear seat belts. "Who would want to steal it," Appa laughed whenever Umma asked him to lock the car.

Appa drove the Tank to the Korean Presbyterian Church in Sacramento where other Korean immigrants gathered to socialize and support one another. "Others can tell we're the most recent immigrants by what type of car we drive," Appa stated. "Look, Mr. Hwang is driving his Mercedes Benz. He has been in the States since the late sixties," Appa said with envy. "Look over there, on your right; it is Mr. Sim. He owns a janitorial business, and employs many immigrants from Korea. Maybe he will let us clean one or two buildings to supplement our income," Appa exclaimed to Umma. She smiled at Appa with a hopeful look before Appa noted, "Mr. Sim is getting out of his blue Mercedes. Mrs. Sim drove her own black Mercedes."

"They must be really rich." I speculated in a loud voice.

"They must be," Umma acknowledged in a defeated tone. As we parked our car among the expensive cars in the church parking lot, I felt really poor for the first time in my life. Before then, I hadn't recognized the difference between rich and poor.

"Let's go in," Appa added hurriedly. I didn't want to go in. It was a long walk from the parking lot to the front door of the church, so I dragged behind my family. "Hurry up," Appa impatiently demanded, "You are always so slow." From the outside, the church looked small. Inside I was surprised to see how large the sanctuary was and how many people were seated. Almost everyone there was Korean, but there were also a few Caucasian men with their Korean wives. The Pastor spoke only in Korean. My parents called him Pastor Yi. He was a very humble man. He had one son and two daughters, all of them teenagers. The daughters were kind to my family and welcomed us to the church. After the service, we went to the greeting room and met a few other Korean families.

After the service, the church served *kimchi*, rice, and seaweed for lunch. It was wonderful to eat *kimchi* made from Napa cabbage because the only *kimchi* we had been able to eat since arriving in America was made of yellowish-green cabbage. Umma had tried to buy some Napa cabbage at a local grocery store, but they didn't stock any.

After lunch, we drove home in the Green Tank. For the first time, I was embarrassed to be in our car as the Green Tank looked older and uglier than it had earlier that morning. Suddenly, I was comparing our family to other families, something I'd never done before and that made me feel incredibly sad.

When we got back from church, Umma let us go play further away from our apartment than usual. "Why don't you kids go out and play and make new friends," Umma declared with an enthusiastic expression on her face. After visiting the Korean church, Umma felt sorry for us because she couldn't give us material things.

There were two playgrounds at the Rosewood Apartments. Everywhere I turned that particular

Sunday afternoon, children were playing, crowding both playgrounds and even the parking lot.

Our apartment was upstairs, and climbing the stairs was really fun. I had never seen apartments before coming to America. In front of our building, there was a huge mulberry tree, so we put a rope around it to make a swing.

One day, my brother, sisters and I were playing outside when we met two dark-skinned children who wanted to play with us. I had never seen African American children before. They were smiling at us and speaking to us, but I couldn't understand them, though I could tell they were friendly. Despite the language barrier, we were able to easily play together.

Later, I found out their names were Chicken and Babe. These were their nicknames, but I didn't know that at the time, and I never learned their real names. Chicken was Babe's older brother. The two boys had several brothers and one sister, all of whom lived in their grandmother's apartment. Their father had killed their mother, so their grandmother did what she could to raise them. The boys were very nice, and I found out later that they were really popular at school. They protected me from bullies, and I got to know them more and more every day.

Life seemed like it was moving really slowly as the days felt long and tiresome. In Korea, we had risen early in the morning and worked until dark. But in America, I played with new friends everyday from late morning to evening. I did this all summer long from May until early September.

There was not much to do around the apartments, and I was scared to go outside without my two older sisters. But one day, Chicken and Babe asked if Jin-bok and I wanted to walk to a shopping center on Kiefer Boulevard for some ice cream. "Are you sure we can leave the apartment without telling Umma," I asked Jin-bok with caution. I was worried, but I went since Jin-bok was going. I thought that she was tough and scary looking, so I felt as though nothing could happen to me.

With only a few cents in our pockets, we left the apartment buildings and walked for what felt like miles and miles toward the shopping center on Kiefer Boulevard. I was nervous, yet curious to see what was outside of the apartment buildings. To my surprise, I saw many new and wonderful things, such as fruit and nut trees around people's homes. Some people had small homes on large lots with lots of open space; the homes were nothing like those I knew in Korea. These homes were a lot closer to each other with flat and clean roofs, while some Korean roofs had Korean squashes or other gourds growing on them. The black streets were clean and smooth with white lines to divide traffic. It seemed like everything was perfectly in order.

In Korea, the roads were bumpy and uneven. I'd only seen a few trucks, and hardly ever saw small family cars. Here, I saw trucks, buses, cars, and motorcycles almost everywhere I looked. I had never seen a motorcycle before, and I found them fascinating.

After passing a few streets, we finally arrived at the shopping center, a big lot with many stores and many cars parked in rows. We walked into a store called Thrifty, and inside the store, there were bright lights everywhere. There were things you could buy that I had never seen before, like fingernail polish, make-up, and cat and dog food. In Korea, the cats and dogs ate things around the farm. I don't recall Umma ever giving the farm animals special food.

Chicken and Babe took us to the ice cream section. I was amazed that there were so many different flavors to choose from. The colors were very bright and beautiful. I did not know which one to choose. I opted for the green ice cream because green was my favorite color. I did not know how to ask for the ice cream, so I just pointed to the one I wanted.

The lady behind the plastic window asked, "Mint

chocolate chip?" I just nodded my head in agreement.

She gave me one scoop of mint chocolate chip ice cream in a cone. I took the cone and gave her a dime. I looked at the ice cream and did not know how to eat it.

I watched as the other children ate theirs, licking it with their tongues and eating the cones after they were done with the ice cream. They smiled as they ate. I closed my eyes and took the first lick of my mint chocolate chip ice cream. It was cold. It tasted bitter at first, and then really sweet. It was creamy, too. I knew why the children smiled while they ate their ice cream. On that day, it did feel a little bit like heaven to be in America. I had never tasted ice cream before, and it was so yummy. I still remember the sensation after so many years and to this day, mint chocolate chip is still my favorite ice cream flavor.

We walked back to the Rosewood Apartments eating our ice cream along the way. This time the walk didn't seem long at all. When we got home, I thanked

Chicken and Babe for taking us, and they smiled back at us, so I guessed they were happy to have us as their new friends. I pointed to our home and waved good-bye. It was dusk, so when we got home, Umma had our dinner ready. After dinner I told Umma and my other siblings what Jin-bok and I had eaten. I told them about the texture and the flavor of the mint chocolate chip.

Jin-hun and Jin-suk didn't say much, but my sister Jeong-mi proclaimed, "I want ice cream too." I told her that I would take her the next time we went. We continued to talk about all the fun and new things we'd seen during the day. When it was time to go to sleep, I washed and lay down next to my siblings. I couldn't sleep right away. I was still thinking about the mint chocolate chip ice cream and hoping to get some more very soon.

Chapter 19

Stacey

The day after Labor Day in 1978, I went to my fourth grade class. It was my first day of school in America. I was nervous and excited at the same time. I'd been looking forward to school since I hadn't done much reading or writing over the summer. I'd only learned a little bit of English from friends at the Rosewood Apartments. I was eager to make new friends and to learn to read and write in English.

On that first day of school, Umma was up early. She got us up and fed us a Korean–style breakfast: rice with vegetable soup, side dishes of *kimchi*, and several layers of toasted seaweed. None of us had new clothes, only what we'd brought from Korea. As we put on our nicest clothes, we discovered that they were too short or too small. We'd all grown over the summer. I put on a long, pink blouse that was made of wrinkle-free nylon that I'd worn to school in Korea, with a polyester navy pleated skirt. Unfortunately, my blouse was too short in the arms, and the skirt was too high on my thighs.

I cried for new clothes saying, "Umma, why can't I have new clothes?"

"Sami, please don't cry," Umma said. "We don't have any money to buy new clothes, nor do I know where to get them." There was a strained tone to Umma's voice.

I was upset and embarrassed, but I didn't have any other option but to wear what I had. Appa, Umma, and Komo drove us all to school in our Green Tank. All eight of us fit in the car, including Komo who had come to translate for my parents. As we drove from our apartment, I noticed Chicken and Babe taking a school bus. Appa followed the bus as he hadn't been sure where to go.

We finally arrived at our new school and got out of the Green Tank to walk to the office with our parents and Komo. My two older sisters, Unni and Jin-bok, had come with us too, waiting patiently. After we registered, we were taken to our classrooms.

When I opened the door to my classroom, I saw boys and girls my age, all looking at me. My very first American teacher was Mrs. Barbara Spencer. She was short with white hair pulled back with black hairpins, beautiful blue eyes, and thin pink-red lips.

"Well, good morning everyone," she announced, "It is very nice to meet all of you. My name is Mrs. Spencer. I will be your fourth grade teacher this year. We will learn everyone's names together, but before we do that, I would like to introduce all of you to our new student from Korea."

Mrs. Spencer gestured for me to come to the

front of the classroom. I got up shyly; I was frightened, nervous, and embarrassed as I didn't like people staring at me. I put my head down and looked at the floor and my black shoes. A few moments passed, and when I looked up, everyone was still staring at me. I didn't know what to say, so I smiled with a half grin. I could feel my face heating up and my heart pumping faster. Finally, Mrs. Spencer pointed to my desk, and I sat back down. I'd only been standing in front of the classroom for a couple of minutes, but it had felt like hours. It was a relief to sit down on my little chair with my desk in front of me. My desk was very smooth on top, and it had a place to put papers and pencils. The classroom had a green chalkboard with the alphabet written along the top of it, one sink in the back of the room, a long countertop, and several north-facing windows. Below the windows, there were more countertops to place books or art projects. The room was perpetually bright with sunlight streaming in and encompassing all corners of the classroom.

I patiently listened to what Mrs. Spencer said, but I could not understand a thing; it just sounded like noise. Eventually, the bell rang, and all the students went outside for recess, a time to go outdoors and play. The playground was wide open with a small baseball field and a large soccer field, and enclosed by plum trees and peach trees.

Back on the playground, there was a large green wall with dodge ball stands, poles for tetherball, and a few basketball courts. No one played basketball since most of us were still too short. I had no clue as to what activity to engage in. I followed the others girls and copied what they did at recess.

A little girl came up to me and said, "Hi, my name is Stacey Rogers." I just looked at her and smiled since I could not understand. I figured she was introducing herself or asking if I wanted to play with her, so I nodded my head and smiled. Little by little, I was able to understand what she was communicating by watching her body language, and soon I was able to pronounce her name. She was unfailingly kind with a dark, inviting face with African features. She was short and skinny with very curly hair that I'd never seen before in Korea.

After school, Jin-hun, Jeong-mi, and I rode the school bus home as some of our new friends had helped us learn how to ride it. Riding the bus home was exhilarating as I had never ridden one back in Korea. From that day on, Stacey helped me acclimate to the new school and taught me how to pronounce different words and the names of other children in the classroom. Soon, others joined in teaching me their names. It wasn't long before I was able to play on the playground without feeling uncomfortable or frustrated from not being able to understand. Every day got a little easier as I learned how to communicate with other children.

Stacey made me feel welcome in the United States. She taught me to love and trust, and not to be afraid to talk to someone who was different than I was, especially if they spoke another language.

Chapter 20

Sixth Grade

I don't remember neither my fifth grade teacher nor the classroom at all. However, I do remember my sixth grade teacher, Mr. Alquist, vividly. He had dark brown hair and a long, brown beard on his face. For me, sixth grade began in September of 1980. The classroom had several north-facing windows and a green chalkboard facing east.

From Mr. Alquist's classroom, I was able to see the soccer field, the baseball field, and parts from the playground. Sometimes, I would look out and daydream instead of listening to Mr. Alquist since I couldn't understand him very well. While I was better at understanding English, I was still struggling to read and write, and my family was still too poor to hire tutors.

Mr. Alquist screamed at the students, especially the boys, when they misbehaved badly, talking over him, or refusing to listen to him. I remembered Mr. Alquist turning red in the face from yelling and screaming so forcefully. It seemed like he was screaming more often than he was teaching, and the boys thought this was funny. Once, he picked up a desk and threw it across the room at a boy who was not listening.

Sometimes, there were boys that talked back to Mr. Alquist. This was a new concept to me. In South Korea, students gave their teachers the utmost respect, raising their hands when they wanted to speak and waiting for the teachers to call on them. I realized that in the United States, students had a lot of power. They felt entitled to talk back to their teachers or even talk down to them. I could never talk back to my teachers like that, as I had far too much respect for them, so this lack of respect left me utterly confused.

During the summer of 1980, I made some new Korean friends named Moon-hee, Joo-hee, Sun-hee, and Mi-sun. They only spoke Korean, similar to when I first arrived in America. I was closest to Moon-hee and Joo-hee as they were in Mr. Alquist's class. We often helped each other navigate the English lessons.

We all lived in the same apartment building off of Kiefer Boulevard. I saw my Korean friends after school, and we played together as much as we could before each of us had to help our parents clean office buildings at night.

Joo-hee, Moon-hee, and I often played on the playgrounds around the apartment building. Sometimes, I went to play with Joo-hee and her three younger brothers, Tae-jun, Tae-hun, and Doe-han, while their parents worked at the Oki Nursery with my parents.

Joo-hee lived two doors down, and our parents often talked a lot about raising children in America and the struggles they were facing. Joo-hee was the only daughter of Mr. and Mrs. Yi. She had to take care of her three younger brothers while the parents went to work cleaning office buildings, just as my parents did. Sometimes they also went to help their parents clean. We were both only twelve at the time.

Joo-hee cooked and cleaned for her three younger brothers while she studied. All four of them studied very hard in school and worked tirelessly at night helping their parents, and as a result, they were some of the immigrant children who did well in school. Joo-hee's father stressed that education was vitally important. This sentiment was a result of the fact that both parents had been educated in Korea.

Moon-hee was the youngest of four children. She had one older sister and two older brothers. Her parents, Mr. and Mrs. Pae, were a lot older than my parents. They lived across the apartment building, but later bought a house. Since Moon-hee's three older siblings had been educated in South Korea, they quickly adjusted to life in the United States. They also had cousins living in America for several years, who were able to help them with their English.

The first time I met Moon-hee was at a playground in our apartment complex. Her hair was short and straight in the front and long and curly in the back. She wore a long-sleeved green top and blue jeans.

In sixth grade, Joo-hee, Moon-hee, and the rest of the class went to Sly Park near Apple Hill. Sly Park hosted sixth graders from all over California in order to teach them about the outdoors and Native Americans. There would be a whole week of making new friends, building stronger relationships, and creating a lifetime of memories. With sheer excitement, I packed a sleeping bag and other items that I needed for the trip. However, I was really scared as I had never been away from both of my parents at the same time, but I still wanted to go with my classmates. My family didn't have enough money to send me, but somehow they managed by saving cans and newspapers and selling the vegetables Umma grew near the apartment buildings. My roommates were going to be Moon-hee, Joo-hee, and Mi-sun.

When it was time to leave for Sly Park, we all hugged and cried with our parents. We rode on a yellow school bus toward Lake Tahoe. The trip lasted about an hour and a half. This was my first time in the mountains since moving to America. It was a cool day in May and I saw many pine trees lined up like fences that divided the American homes in Sacramento, and like those back in South Korea up in the mountains. My sister, Jin-bok and I used to climb the trees to get pine needles to burn during winter months. The sky was filled with the puffy blue and white clouds like the cotton balls that I saw when our family flew into San Francisco Airport from Hawaii.

When we reached our destination, everyone

became excited. Three other elementary schools were there at the same time, so the camp was filled to the brim with children. We had adult leaders and parent volunteers with us for the whole week as well. The girls and boys were placed in separate cabins, though we shared cabin space with students from other schools. Everyone was happy and kind.

After we were shown to our cabins, we left our belongings and went to meet other students in the cafeteria. The cafeteria was huge, the food was great, and the portions were generous. Breakfast was served at 7:00 a.m., lunch at 11:00 a.m., and dinner at 5:00 p.m. Lights were out by 9:00 p.m., so we had to carry flashlights to use the restrooms.

Many activities were planned for us. We went on hiking trips to see birds and the lake, and we were even allowed to swim in the lake. It was still cool at Sly Park, and snow was still melting around us. As I was hiking, I saw many pinecones and pine needles like I had in

Korea. I wanted to collect them like I had done during the winter in Korea, but I realized that I didn't have to do that anymore. I was just allowed to be a kid and enjoy nature. It was a strange feeling, and I felt guilty for enjoying it, but I kept that to myself.

After hiking, we came back to the camp and had a huge lunch. Later, we were given a choice of different activities. For example, we could make necklaces with Native American beads or learn to weave baskets and cloth.

We also had a worm-eating contest. To my surprise, there were many kids that ate worms, especially the boys. The girls screamed when they saw boys eating the worms, and some kids even threw up after consumption, but most were fine. I think some of them felt more confident about themselves after that day.

Even though we had a full schedule, we were encouraged to talk with children from other schools. I think that was the best part of the whole trip. I didn't know there were so many other children my age that lived nearby.

I remember one girl, Tracy, in particular. She had blonde hair and blue eyes. I still have her school picture somewhere. We got to know each other and so, we exchanged addresses and wrote to each other a few times, but we lost contact after I moved.

Due to this trip, I also got to know more of my classmates from James W. Marshall Elementary School. Michael was a thin, tall, redheaded boy who was nice to all the Korean kids. I found out that his mother had died of breast cancer. My classmates also included twin brothers, Larry and Gary. Michael and the twins were neighbors. The twins were so smart and unfailingly kind. They had curly blond hair and blue eyes. A lot of girls at our school liked them. I was 12 and it was the first time in my life I'd noticed a boy. I thought Gary was really cute and I found out later that he liked me too. However, after I graduated from sixth grade, I had to move and we lost contact.

We returned to Sacramento on Friday afternoon. My parents were waiting for me at school along with the other parents. They seemed very happy to see me, and I was happy to see them too, but I also knew that starting Monday night, I would be going back to cleaning office buildings with Appa and Umma. I wasn't looking forward to that.

Chapter 21

White Tennis Shoes

In 1981, I entered seventh grade at Albert Einstein Junior High in Sacramento. The day before school started, Appa took me to buy new clothes and tennis shoes. I felt ecstatic since I never went anywhere alone with Appa, nor did I ever go shopping just for myself. Almost all of my clothes had been handed down from my two older sisters, Unni and Jin-bok. Buying new clothes meant I could choose the colors and styles I liked.

Umma stayed home to watch my other siblings. I was relieved when I discovered Umma wouldn't be choosing the color of my clothes because Umma always chose red. Red was her favorite color, and she always expected us to wear it; however, red is one of my least favorite colors.

After lunch, Appa told me to get ready to go shopping. I put on my pink, green, and white sweatsuit that I had bought with my baby-sitting money. I always liked clothes that covered my arms and legs. I just felt more comfortable wearing things that protected my modesty.

After I got dressed, Appa and I got into his new yellow truck. It was Appa's first new car. It only had three seatbelts, but since most of us were thin, we were usually able to sit four across, squeezing into the seats, but leaving no room to move.

Appa and I headed to Rancho Cordova, where my Komo lived. The inside of Appa's truck seemed big to me since I didn't have to share space on this trip. I wished that the feeling of unadulterated joy I felt in that small moment would last forever.

Appa got off Highway 50 at Sunrise Boulevard and headed north. After about a half mile, he turned left on Zinfandel Drive and made another quick right into the parking lot of Kmart. It was a huge parking lot with so many cars. As our truck blended into the sea of Chevys and Fords, I felt like Appa was becoming an American.

This was my first visit to Kmart. I never saw so many lights in one store. The store was filled to the brim with toys and clothes to appease all ages. The shelves were laden with kitchen supplies, furniture, electronics, and cosmetics. The only goods absent from the store were fresh foods like fruits, vegetables, milk, and eggs.

Appa and I wandered around until we found the girls' clothes. As we entered the wonderland of pastel pinks, purple, and creams, I was entranced by all of the beautiful clothing for sale. Appa said I could choose anything I wanted for one outfit. It was not easy to choose, however, as there were so many pretty dresses, coats, jackets, pants, skirts, and tops. The weather was still very hot, so it was difficult to find something that fulfilled my desire to stay covered. Eventually, I saw a beautiful beige long sleeved top. Adorned with a handsome lace collar, the top felt luxurious between my fingers, like soft velvet. To accompany my new top, I opted for matching beige pants. After we purchased my new outfit, Appa and I went to Kinney Shoes on Folsom Boulevard. With heels, sneakers, flats, and sandals scattered throughout the store, I concluded that I had never seen so many shoes in my life. From sparkly stilettos to rugged mountain boots, there were shoes catering to men, women, boys, girls, and even babies.

Appa took me to the aisle with tennis shoes and told me to choose one pair. I couldn't believe this was happening. I was so excited, yet I felt guilty that I was the only one there at the store. At that time, I didn't know that Appa had done this for all of my siblings.

I chose the whitest tennis shoes available because

they looked so beautiful and bright. They were my first new tennis shoes, and I cherished them dearly.

By the time we got home, it was close to dinnertime. While Umma was getting things ready for dinner, my siblings gathered around to look at my new outfit.

Once Umma announced that dinner was ready, we went into the small kitchen to eat on the floor rather than on chairs. We didn't have enough chairs for all eight of us unless we rotated, and that would have been difficult since most of us were young and hungry all the time.

After dinner was over, Umma told us to wash and get ready for school in the morning. This was a challenge since we only had one full bathroom upstairs and one powder room with a sink and toilet downstairs. Still, we felt blessed. Just a few years before, we'd had only one bathroom for the whole family.

I was so excited about going to junior high school

that I couldn't sleep at all. I didn't know if the eighth and ninth graders were going to be nice to me or force me to do things I didn't want to do, like smoking cigarettes. With so many thoughts littering my mind, I continually tossed and turned in my bed. I got up and tried on my new clothes and tennis shoes in an effort to ease my mind, but my sisters kept telling me to turn off the light. I finally fell asleep after midnight.

When I awakened the next morning, my new clothes and white tennis shoes were resting beside my head where I'd left them. I was the first one to dress. After Umma fed us breakfast, I left home, brimming with excitement, and met Joo-hee and Moon-hee to travel to school together on our first day as junior high students.

Chapter 22

Dreaming in English

When I was in the seventh grade, a friend, Daphne, asked me if I dreamt in English or in Korean. I'd never thought about it until that moment and it was on my mind for the rest of the day. I asked several of my Korean friends if they dreamt in English, and most said they dreamt only in Korean.

I went home and thought about it all night. I couldn't sleep, so I asked my siblings if they dreamt in English or in Korean. The younger ones, like Jin-hun, Jeong-mi, and Jin-suk, claimed that they dreamt only in English while my two older sisters, Unni and Jin-bok, dreamt only in Korean. I thought it was amazing that six of us under the same roof were dreaming in two different languages.

It stayed on my mind for several days, and I couldn't sleep well. During that time, dreams were absent from my nights.

One evening, I finally had a dream in which the voices were speaking in English. Ever since then, I've dreamt only in English. I remember that when I first came to America in the fourth grade, I was dreaming only in Korean. I did all my multiplication and everything else in my head in Korean. I don't know why the switch happened to me and not to my older sisters, perhaps it was because I had started learning English before I was twelve. To this day, my two older sisters still dream only in Korean.

Recently, I was talking with a boy who spoke three languages fluently. I asked him which language he dreamt in. He told me it depended on which language he spoke earlier that day. He dreams in all three languages, but not at the same time.

Some day I want to dream in Korean again. While it hasn't happened yet, if I speak and think in Korean all day, perhaps I will finally dream in my native tongue.

Chapter 23

Learning by the Bible

When I was in the middle of seventh grade, my family moved to Stockton, California. Appa found another job cleaning office buildings in downtown Stockton, he wanted to move our family mainly for Jin-bok's sake. Appa wanted her to meet new friends and start over as he felt Jin-bok's friends were a bad influence on her. I think Appa liked running away. He constantly yearned to move to new towns, never wanting to settle in one place. He never asked what Umma or his children wanted; he simply made a decision, and we followed him.

Jin-bok and I went to work every night, Monday

through Friday, to help Appa and Umma clean office buildings. My parents needed us to translate the notes from English to Korean that the offices left for us. Many nights I didn't want to go with them, but I knew Appa and Umma needed me. They would say, "Sami, you need to come with us every night so that we can finish our work earlier. You need to translate English to Korean, so that we don't throw away anything we aren't supposed to."

Appa, Umma, Jin-bok, and I would work late at night cleaning offices: dusting, vacuuming, throwing trash out, and cleaning bathrooms. The work was dirty, and the bathrooms smelled horrible. It was hard work, and it could also be humiliating because I felt some people were viewing us strangely, looking down on us like we were aliens from outer space. At the age of ten, I knew I could not do this for very long.

We started work at around 5:00 p.m. and worked tirelessly until as late as 1:00 a.m. Many nights, after

Jin-bok and I finished our homework, we only had a few hours to sleep before going to school, often sleep-deprived and cranky. I felt embarrassed that we had to clean office buildings because none of my American friends had to do that kind of work. Unlike my peers, I didn't have time to play sports, to learn to play the piano, or to practice ballet. My other friends didn't have parents that were constantly worried about having enough money for food and rent. I worried that my friends would ask me what my parents did for a living, but they never did to my relief. If they had, I don't know what I would have told them. I felt more ashamed of our lives in America than I had ever felt while living and helping Umma on the farm in Korea.

Weekends in Stockton weren't any better than the busy weekdays as I had to spend them cleaning the new home we rented off Hammer Lane. On Sundays, we went to a Korean Christian Church; however, we weren't Christians, so we only went to socialize with other Koreans in Stockton.

One Sunday morning, I decided to take a Bible from the church. I wanted to use it to learn English and to discover God's identity. Appa and Umma never talked about God at home and no one ever prayed.

After I took the Bible home with me, I was stricken with guilt because I knew what I'd done was wrong. Appa and Umma never noticed, and no one ever mentioned it at the church. However, many nights I couldn't sleep because of what I had done. I knew from reading the Bible that stealing was wrong. For as long as I could remember, Umma had told me taking something from someone's yard or garden, even a single piece of fruit, would be reprehensible. I thought it was part of the Korean culture that stealing was wrong, but something in the Bible had made it official. I was scared.

By the time I decided to give the Bible back, we had already moved away from Stockton. I was worried that Appa and Umma would be ashamed of what I had done, or that Appa would spank me for it, so I never told anyone.

From that Bible, I learned a lot about God's laws in addition to many new English words and sentence structure. I became acquainted with the Christian view of world history. Most importantly, I learned that if I didn't love, then I had absolutely nothing.

I found the Bible really interesting because each chapter had its own supporting narratives, illustrating Christian ideology. There were answers to many of the questions I had as a child; for example, the Bible answered why I was on earth, and where I would go when I died.

After I read the whole Bible, my fears about sickness and death disappeared. I decided that everything in my life should be done with love. The Bible had all the answers to my questions and I felt honored that I'd learned to read and write from this place of unyielding love.

Several years later, I revealed to my parents about how I took the Bible from church, but they didn't get upset. When I told a few friends of mine, they informed me that the Bibles at churches were usually free as they wanted people to take them and learn more about Christ. It was a huge relief.

Chapter 24

Third Daughter

When we moved to Stockton in 1981, I changed my name from "Sami" to "Jeannie." I felt embarrassed when people mispronounced my Korean name, and it seemed important to have an American name like everyone else. At the time, I thought American names sounded prettier. Some of my classmates, mostly boys, made fun of my name and I took it personally. I wished that if I had an American girl's name, the seventh-grade boys like Benny would stop making fun of me.

Sometimes, I was so bothered by my classmates' teasing that I didn't want to go to school, but I knew Umma and Appa wouldn't sympathize. They'd most likely be upset with me instead of the other children. If I'd skipped school, I might have even gotten a spanking from Appa, so I kept these troubles to myself.

Umma and Appa were often so busy that they didn't have time to listen to my complaints. I kept my feelings a secret until I discovered that my two older sisters were also considering changing their names.

My older sisters officially changed their names from "Jin-sun" to "Jennifer" and "Jin-bok" to "Sandra." Jennifer's husband, Tony, wanted her to have an American name, and he helped her choose it.

Jin-bok changed her name in the ninth grade. She explained that her decision to adopt the name, "Sandra," was due to the teasing she experienced from her classmates at Albert Einstein Junior High. Sandra took her name from a TV soap opera character. She remembered Sandra, the actress, as being very beautiful, so my sister wanted to look like her.

In Korean, Sami refers to the number three. Umma

named me Sami because I was her third daughter. Umma was supposed to give me a family name that started with "Jin" but she decided not to follow that tradition as "Third Daughter" has a special meaning.

As a third daughter in Korean culture, when a suitor comes to look for a prospective wife, it is said he looks at her hands and feet to see if they are strong and able to work hard. Next, he'll make sure the girl is beautiful. However, when a girl is named "Third Daughter," a suitor will marry the girl without looking at her feet, hands, or face solely because of the name.

Upon arriving in America, the immigration officials spelled my name wrong. It was taken down as "Sam-hui" instead of "Sami." Since Americans commonly have middle names, my classmates thought "Sami" was my first name and "hui" was my middle name. This incident furthered my desire to "Americanize" my name.

I was so excited to choose my own name. Jin-bok had a best friend named Jeannie Alderman, who was so beautiful and so kind that I wanted to be like her. Jeannie was half Filipino and half Caucasian with beautiful dark brown hair and golden skin. Always smiling and seemingly happy, she was genuine in everything she did and said. Jeannie took the time to get to know each of us, and made an effort to stay in contact with Jin-bok even after we moved to Stockton.

After I chose my new name, my siblings started to call me "Jeannie" right away. However, at home, Umma and Appa continued to call me Sami.

Chapter 25

Sink or Swim

Adjusting to American life was easier for me than for Unni and Jin-bok. This could be a result of my young age when we moved to America. I learned to speak, read, and write fairly quickly. Appa and Umma took English courses at night at a local adult school, but they became very frustrated. Appa quickly gave up on learning to read and write in English. He had a difficult time pronouncing L's and R's, and thus relied on his children to translate for him. **As he could not speak, read, or write in English, it was difficult for him to find a well-paying job, so he and Umma stayed with the Oki Nursery longer than they have wanted.**

At night, Jin-bok and I worked with Umma and Appa when we should have been home studying. We would get home at three o'clock in the afternoon, and then eat lunch and do our homework. At around five o'clock, we packed into the Green Tank and headed towards the Teichert and Sons building in North Sacramento. Jin-hun, Jeong-mi, and Jin-suk stayed at home by themselves and waited for our return.

I struggled in school. There was no extra time to study. Some days I complained to Appa and Umma and told them I didn't want to go to work. I knew it hurt them very much as Umma admitted to me that it was humiliating for them to ask their children for help.

I know Umma thought of that quite often because she would say, "I'm not a good mother. I can't help my children do what they want, like learning to play the piano or helping them pay for gymnastics." Umma felt helpless and frustrated with Appa because he was never home and didn't seem to care. I think Appa felt the same frustration; he just didn't know how to express himself as Korean men weren't encouraged to show their emotions.

Some people were nice at the office building where we helped Appa and Umma clean. They asked about our names, ages, and what country we came from. There was one gentleman, Wells Bain, the security guard at the Teichert Building, who was particularly kind to us. He sometimes helped me with my writing assignments. Wells began working there after he retired from his military service; he'd served in both World War I and II. Some days, he would bring his military uniforms from both wars, and show me some magazines and costume jewelry from the 1940s. I still have one of those fashion magazines.

He was an incredible writer. He wrote all the time, especially to the newspapers like the *Sacramento Union* and the *Sacramento Bee*, criticizing things like war and the mistreatment of animals.

However, Wells' kindness was somewhat overshadowed by some of the other workers. A few women in the offices were very mean to my family and me. They would accuse us of stealing or throwing things away that were meant to be saved and make us clean their desks and make us vacuum over and over again while they watched.

My parents weren't working for Teichert and Sons directly. They were working for Mr. Hwang, who owned Tom's Maintenance Company. He spoke English very well, and we respected him greatly as he provided Appa and Umma with jobs. Umma was always happy that we had extra money coming in besides that from the Oki Nursery. However, Mr. Hwang never gave us paid vacation time or holidays. He didn't pay very well, either. Years later, we discovered that Mr. Hwang paid fines for not giving his workers vacation time or holiday pay. However, I never disliked him. In fact, I was always thankful that he gave Appa and Umma work when we really needed help. Unfortunately, Mr. Hwang died from liver cancer at a very young age.

Chapter 26

Bleeding Steak

In 1984, our family moved to Rancho Cordova. Komo and Komobo wanted us to live near them and offered to rent us their old house. In the meantime, Appa found another job cleaning offices in Sacramento. That fall I was going into ninth grade at Mitchell Junior High. We hadn't moved until summer because Appa and Umma wanted me to finish the school year at Lincoln Junior High in Stockton. I'd been enrolled in three different schools in three years, and with all of our moving, I hadn't been able to make many new friends.

It seemed like every time I started to feel comfortable at a new school, we moved. I wanted to complain, but I couldn't. Whenever I asked Appa a question, he would yell at me and tell me to keep my mouth shut. For Appa, a little girl's opinion wasn't worth his consideration. I knew it was disrespectful to question the decisions of a parent or an elder, but Appa never asked us what we wanted. He never consulted with Umma about what was best for their children, making his decisions blindly about where we were going to live and when we would move.

Junior high school was a lot different from elementary school. In elementary school, kids just wanted to make new friends and play games. Beginning in junior high, I noticed kids only hung around with other kids who looked like them. African Americans would congregate mostly with other African Americans. Asian Americans preferred to be with other Asian Americans. I didn't understand this separation as I felt it was important to celebrate our differences. In the most productive environments in the world, each person brings their own cultural ideals and everyone learns from each other's traditions and experiences. Even though our cultures were unique, our feelings, fears, struggles, and pains were universal.

Even my Korean friends just wanted to be around other Koreans. I didn't like the way kids were separating themselves by the way they looked. I wanted to be friends with everyone. Unfortunately, this desire didn't go over well with my Korean friends, who began to ignore me. They called me a "banana," meaning that I looked Asian on the outside, but acted white on the inside. I didn't even know what "acting white" meant. I was hurt and felt left out, and as a result, I distanced myself from other Koreans for a while. Some American kids were just as mean when I hung around my Korean friends, they would tell us to "Speak English," or "Go back to your own country." When people spoke to me in this way, I felt that speaking Korean was a crime.

As a result, I focused on learning English and

making new friends who cared about me.

Komo's house was a small property built in the 1960s. This was the house we slept in on our first night in America, and where we celebrated my tenth birthday.

The walls were covered with wood panels, and the windows were very small. Since we'd first visited the house six years ago, Komo had expanded the family room and built a fireplace. We lived in this house for the next eight years because the rent Komo charged us was cheaper than any other place we could rent.

Appa never wanted to look for another place even though Umma felt very uneasy about renting from Komo. She didn't want to take advantage of Komo. Komo could have made a lot more money if she had rented her house to strangers. Umma figured that Komo felt obligated to help us since she'd sponsored us, and knew her brother wasn't making enough money to support his own family.

Financial arguments were never-ending between

Appa and Umma. Appa never made an effort to save money or to buy his own house, so Umma started to save money on her own. She started to plant fruit trees in the front of the house and vegetables in the back and front yards. Appa would complain about the vegetables planted in the front yard, but eventually he let her do what she wanted. He knew that it gave us plenty of vegetables that Umma didn't need to purchase, relieving some of our financial burden. There was enough produce that Umma even shared the vegetables with Komo and some of our neighbors.

Komo and Komobo bought a new house near Cordova High School. By this time, Unni, my oldest sister, was married and living in Elk Grove. There were only seven of us now. Our house had a master bedroom, three small bedrooms, and two full bathrooms that we desperately needed. We were all quickly growing up, and having four females fighting over two bathrooms was not easy. Appa and Umma slept in one of the smaller bedrooms, Jin-bok had the tiny bedroom near the front door, and Appa combined the master bedroom and another small bedroom into one large room with a bathroom and shower for Jin-hun, Jeong-mi, Jin-suk, and me to share.

Our bedroom had three windows facing north. We needed the windows since the room was fairly dark. The house was getting old, and the walls were dirty. The carpets weren't any better. However, we tried to appreciate our new home to the best of our ability.

My poor Umma always looked so sad, and I often wondered what she was feeling. She complained to Appa about our living situation, but Appa was frequently out of the house. He was in a no-win situation; he couldn't speak English well enough to get a better paying job, but getting a better job and more cash flow were the only way we could get out of Komo's house and into our own home. It was a hard time for Umma. She didn't have anyone that she could talk to or ask for help. All of her siblings were back in Korea. She didn't know how to speak English, so the only thing she could do was to trust Appa and Komo to make the best decisions for the family.

Umma started to turn the soil in the backyard and front yard during the spring and summer. She harvested a small crop in the fall that included Korean radishes, green onions, and Korean herbs. She kept some for us and sold the rest to the Korean store on Kiefer Boulevard. Mr. Jung, who owned the Korean store, was very nice and always helped her. Sometimes Umma only made fifty cents for a bundle of radishes, but after many bundles, it added up. Umma was always thinking ahead considering she had six children to feed and a husband who wasn't bringing in much income. I don't remember Appa ever working in the backyard or front yard. It was Umma's hard work and resourcefulness that kept us afloat.

While most weekends were spent cleaning the

family home, some days we were allowed to go out and play. Jin-bok, Jeong-mi, and Jin-hun made countless new friends quickly. I made some new friends as well including Andy. She had dark skin and curly black hair just like my friend, Stacey. Andy lived a few houses away. We found out that we were going into the same grade at the same school and became good friends immediately. Andy had lived in Rancho Cordova for many years, so she knew a lot of people. We saw each other almost every day. Unfortunately, we didn't stay good friends for long. She constantly borrowed money from me and would never pay it back. It was always a small amount, but it started to add up. I figured she would pay me back as that was what I did even when I borrowed a few cents from friends. I reimbursed my friends the very next day and if I didn't, I couldn't sleep. Umma always reminded me not to borrow money from people, warning, "Sami, if you borrow money you may get into a habit of doing so, and you may continue to do that as an adult. It is easy to borrow money, but very hard to pay it back."

After a while, I figured out that Andy wasn't really a good friend. I don't hold any grudges against her today, but it was a good lesson for me to learn—not to let people borrow money unless I was willing to give it to them as a gift.

Andy introduced me to others like Robyn, who became a good friend of mine for many years. Robyn was tall and skinny with blonde hair and blue eyes. One day, Andy, Robyn, and I walked a few miles away from home to Kmart where Robyn wanted to meet a guy friend, Toby. He had long brown hair, hazel eyes, and a very nice tan. Toby was Hawaiian, French, and Irish. Robyn really liked him, and they talked for a while. After they chatted, I think they kissed, too. I didn't say very much to Toby, as I was shy and I didn't really know him, but Andy seemed to know him really well. She told me about how many girls at school liked him and how he was so popular. After Robyn finished talking with Toby, we said our good–byes, and he rode off on his bike toward Sunrise Boulevard.

The summer of 1984 felt short, but Andy and Robyn kept me busy with lots of talk about boys. Too soon, the summer ended, and we had to go back to school.

School was only a few minutes away. I lived behind the campus near the track and field area. The very first day at Mitchell Junior High, I was nervous. The buildings and classrooms looked old, and I had to learn so much about new teachers, new classrooms, and where everything was located. The school seemed very large on that first day. As the weeks went by, it seemed to grow smaller and became easier to navigate. Some of the students looked older than fourteen or fifteen. I noticed a lot of the girls were busy making themselves look pretty and more mature looking. Instead of studying, many of them spent time gushing over boys.

It was hard not to hear them talk about the boys. I didn't say much even though I wanted to fit in as quickly as possible.

I followed Andy around a lot and found out that Robyn and Toby were attending the same school. Those were the only students I knew in my grade. Toby did not talk to me much, just a casual "Hi," whenever he ran into me at school. However, Robyn and I got to know each other better. She was really pretty and very nice. I noticed that a lot of boys at our school liked her.

Another friend that I grew close to during junior high was Kay. Her dad was Caucasian and her mother was Chinese. Kay almost looked like the pop star Madonna. She had brown hair and greenish-brown eyes, like Toby's. Similar to Robyn, she was quite pretty and popular. I met her through Jin-bok. At that time, Jin-bok was dating a boy named James. James and Kay were friends and hung out a lot.

I often went over to Kay's house with Jin-bok. I

met some of Kay's friends, like Dean. Dean was really cute and nice. He had curly, blond hair and blue eyes. I later found out that Toby was his best friend. Almost all of Kay's friends listened to rock music, like AC/DC, Bon Jovi, and Van Halen. Most of them had long hair, especially the guys. I wasn't used to seeing boys with long hair. Some of them also wore dark eyeliner. They looked tough and unapproachable from a distance, but most of them were nice once I got to know them. They did not judge me based on my appearance, perhaps as these boys were used to being judged or misunderstood because of their clothing and accessory choices.

Ninth grade was a challenging year for me. I wanted to fit in so badly. I yearned to be an American and be like other American kids at school. However, I had other responsibilities. No one in my school knew that I cleaned office buildings at night with my parents, and I felt ashamed. Other students were busy talking about boys, and maybe trying out for sports teams like track and field or soccer, but I couldn't do any of those as I knew my parents would not let me.

A few times I told my parents I needed to stay home to do homework. Instead, I played with some of my school friends. When Appa found out what I was doing, I wasn't allowed to stay home anymore.

Months later, Appa finally let me go over to a friend's house. Lisa invited me to meet her parents. She had long, straight blonde hair, and pretty big, blue eyes. She had recently moved to Rancho Cordova and lived on Zinfandel Drive.

Her parents were very nice people; however, I cannot recall their names. After several hours of talking about boys, Lisa and I went to her kitchen to eat dinner. Unbeknownst to me, I would have to eat a steak that was still bleeding.

They served mashed potatoes and green beans with the steak. I ate the potatoes and green beans first and they were really tasty. I thought I was going to die after eating the bleeding steak, but I didn't want to be rude. I didn't know what to do, so I just ate it, struggling to chew and swallow the beef. After eating the steak, I just waited for death to greet me.

Of course, I didn't die, but I was shocked. In our family, I was taught never to eat bleeding meat. I had never seen anyone eat rare meat before. After dinner, I thanked Lisa's parents for dinner and walked back home. After I got home, I told Appa and Umma that I'd had bleeding steak and that I didn't' become ill. I was waiting to have a bad stomachache that night, but I didn't. Despite experiencing no side effects after eating the rare meat, I didn't eat a bleeding steak again for many years.

Chapter 27

Cordova Lancers

In 1985, I went into tenth grade at Cordova High School, home of the Cordova Lancers. The school colors were red, white, and black. Unfortunately, Cordova didn't have many Asian Americans or other minority groups. Most of the students had established their friendships during childhood. It was difficult for recent immigrants to make new friends; thus, it took me a few months to establish a couple of friendships.

By the time I entered high school, I was beginning to feel more comfortable speaking English. Some people at my high school didn't know that English was my second language. They would even say, "Jeannie, you don't have an accent." At first I felt proud to be like one of them, but that feeling didn't last very long.

For my friends, the most exciting thing about being a high school student was being in the tenth grade and getting invited to go to the Junior Prom. The girls talked about it for weeks, discussing possible dates, gowns, and hairstyles for the evening. I was curious and wanted to go to dance with a date like my friends, but my parents would not let me.

"Sami, Korean girls do not go dancing on dates before marriage."

I told them it would only be for one night of the year. I promised to go with several other girlfriends who didn't have dates either, but they still wouldn't let me go. It reminded me that I was different from my American friends. Our family was separated from other families by profound social and cultural differences.

When my best friend, Robyn, turned sixteen, her parents gave her permission to have a boyfriend.

This would never be allowed at my house. On some level, I felt ashamed to be a Korean. My parents were trying to protect me from losing my Korean identity, but they didn't know how to express their frustrations. It still isn't common for Korean fathers to express their feelings to their children. Appa and Umma forced me to stay at home after school. I couldn't participate in sports or go to the movies nor could I go shopping or attend sleepovers.

Because of all my parents' restrictions, I couldn't help but feel I was being held back from becoming an American. I desperately wanted to show my American friends that I was no different from them. Part of me wanted to stay a dutiful daughter, but another part wanted to free myself from my obligations to my family and culture.

Appa was resistant to adopting American culture, but he was fighting a losing battle. My siblings and I only spoke English at home. We could still communicate with our parents, but we were using our Korean less and less. We began losing our mother language.

This bothered our parents. Many times Appa told me that he felt useless, unimportant, and nonexistent, and I felt sorry for him. I'm sure he had many dreams for his children, but what Appa wanted for his children and what his children wanted were two different things.

Robyn and I became best friends in the tenth grade. We spent a lot of time together. Once, I went hiking with her and her father up at Ice House near Lake Tahoe. Another time, Appa took Robyn and me to Lake Tahoe to see the snow.

The first time I cut school was with Robyn. We went to the Florin Mall in Sacramento. At first, I was scared, but I desperately wanted to fit in at school and experience American life. Robyn wanted to skip class because she did not like going to school. She was having problems there and at home with her parents. When I saw her argue with her parents for the first time, I was startled. In Korean culture, children are forbidden from arguing with their parents. However, it struck a chord in me, and I began wondering what it would be like to argue with Appa and Umma.

Appa and Umma didn't like me arguing one bit. I was not the first to challenge them as Jin-bok had done a few years previously. I was already letting this new culture change me, a culture that Appa and Umma didn't want to understand and perhaps couldn't.

I wanted to have blonde hair and blue eyes like Robyn. I wanted to dress up and wear make-up at school. After school, I washed all the make-up off my face to hide my transgression from my parents. I began to rebel more often. I felt conflicted, unable to figure out how to become a real American and retain my Korean roots. I looked in the mirror, and I saw an Asian face. I was ashamed of my Asian looks. I just couldn't explain why I felt this way as I didn't feel ugly. I didn't have anyone I could talk to about these things, and I felt very alone. The whole three years I was at Cordova High, I didn't tell anyone how I felt. Another thing I didn't tell my girl friends was about my menstrual delay. I didn't start until I was 15 years old. Most of my girlfriends started when they were 12 years old. I was embarrassed to tell them that I was still a girl. This is what Umma told me. The day I started was during a weekend and I went to the bathroom since I felt like I needed to go. I sat down to urinate and was ready to flush the toilet when I saw the blood inside the bowl. I screamed for Umma, and she rushed in to see what was wrong with me. When I told her and showed her the blood, she smiled and said, "Oh! This means you're not a little girl anymore" and she left the bathroom. I felt strange and still scared. This was the first time Umma told me to stay away from boys, or I would get pregnant even if I sat next to them.

Sometimes, Appa and Umma manipulated me into staying close to them. They were afraid to lose me. I was still their translator at work and at home. I helped them pay their bills, fill out medical papers, and write their correspondence.

I used to tell Umma that she was stupid, questioning why she was unable to read in Korean or English. I didn't understand how intensely those words might hurt her feelings.

Later, I found that my maternal Weh-Harabaji's father had forbidden his daughters, granddaughters, and great granddaughters to be educated. My great-grandfather didn't allow the females in his family to be educated, but his wife, my great-grandmother, was a very educated lady. She was of the *yangban* class and a part of Jeon-ju Yi Si family. The Jeon-ju Yi Si ruled Korea from 1392 to 1910. When the Japanese occupied Korea on August 22, 1910, it ended the Joseon Dynasty. Kwan Seo-noak brought her own servants with her when she married my Weh Harabaji's father. My great-grandfather was a *seonbi*, a teacher in Yesan,

Chungcheongnam-do.

My educated great-grandmother was not a good housewife. The servants did most of the cooking, washing, and farming, as well as guarding the gate and burning wood to keep the floors warm for the *yangbans*. As a result, she didn't know how to cook or take care of her husband and their children. All she did was read, write poems, and create beautiful *hanja*, Chinese calligraphy. From then on, my great-grandfather forbade all the females in his house from receiving an education so that they could focus on being good wives and mothers. He had his sons marry *yangban* women who were not educated, and thus my Umma was never allowed to make her own decisions regarding her education.

In those days, Korea didn't have public schools. *Seonbi* taught the male *yangban* children at home. The servants and their children weren't allowed to be educated, only the male *yangban* offspring.

Umma never revealed these aspects of her life until I was an adult. She said, "What is the use? We live in America now. Everyone in America is equal. It doesn't matter if you are a *yangban* or a servant. What matters in America is who has money."

During my junior year at Cordova High, a Korean small business owner on Folsom Boulevard in Korea town told Umma to enter me into the Miss Korea competition in San Francisco. She promised to have other small business owners sponsor me. I was so excited by the possibility when Umma discussed the arrangements with Appa.

Appa proclaimed, "No. Sami is still too young and too skinny. She can't speak Korean well. She has no boobs." He wielded so much power over the opportunities in my life, and I started to feel like I was trapped. He had always been such a selfish person. Did he have any of my interests at heart? I couldn't trust him and began to resent him. I started to lie to my parents about a lot of things to avoid getting into trouble.

I felt ashamed and needed to discuss my feelings, but at Cordova High School there were hardly any other Koreans with whom I could relate. One day I met a Korean-American girl named Sandra. I was excited until she called me a "banana." She did not like me one bit, despising the fact that I only had American friends.

Sandra threatened to beat me up after school, so I told Robyn about Sandra and she told me not to worry, stating that she would fight for me. I've never forgotten her kindness. Her comforting words that day are forever ingrained in my memory. Unfortunately, after the eleventh grade, Robyn and I started to grow apart. Eventually, Robyn moved to another school, and I made other friends.

Chapter 28

American River College

After high school, I didn't have a plan about my future. I applied to a local junior college, American River College in Citrus Heights and was accepted. While attending school, I worked at Lerner New York in the Sunrise Mall; Kim's Gift Shop in Rancho Cordova; and the Graphic Arts Department at American River College. I was trying to earn enough to cover my books and tuition. Sometimes, during Christmas vacation, I worked longer hours.

Appa and Umma bought me a new car, a brown Chevy Cavalier. Before that, I took the bus from Rancho Cordova to Citrus Heights, which sometimes took hours.

I started to think about running my own business. I saw that no matter how hard Appa and Umma worked they could never get ahead. This was in part due to the fact that Appa was awful at managing his money. Appa always told Umma, "When I make enough money, I will buy you a house."

Umma heard these words often, but a costly emergency always seemed to drain their funds at the last moment. Appa wasn't able to buy a house until 1993 when he bought a house in Greenhaven in South Sacramento. He was only able to do this with the help of Mrs. Overton, his friend who owned Sunset Cleaners in Sacramento as she let Appa borrow the money.

In college, I had a difficult time with Appa. I was trying to figure out what I wanted to do with my life. I'd always wanted to be a fashion designer since I was ten years old, but Appa and Umma didn't support me in anything related to fashion. I wasn't able to apply to any universities because I didn't have high grades or SAT scores, and I was still struggling with my English skills. Sometimes I felt inferior because Korean mothers gossiped and bragged about their children: how smart they were, what colleges they attended, what types of jobs they had, and who they married.

The Korean mothers in Sacramento treated Appa and Umma badly. Their daughters, Unni and Jin-bok, married non-Koreans, which made heads turn in the Korean community. The Korean mothers gossiped, "Koreans should marry Koreans. When they don't, it is the parents' fault for not teaching their children about their Korean heritage and obligation," or "What sort of parents can't control their own children?" Some Koreans would even poke fun at Unni and Jin-bok for not marrying Koreans. Jin-bok didn't hang around other Koreans because they gave her a hard time about being darker-skinned.

Umma said to us, "Parents should never say bad

things about other children. You never know what your own children might become when they grow older." Alternatively, Appa blamed his children for every negative thing that happened to our family. He often cursed Unni for marrying a non-Korean, believing she was the reason his other children dated and married other non-Koreans. To this day, he still blames her for the misfortunes in his life and the mistakes of all his children, including my failed first marriage.

In 1989, a run of bad luck would change my relationship with Appa permanently. I was still attending American River College and had one semester left. I was set to transfer to the University of California, Davis to major in textiles and design. Appa attended my orientation at UC Davis, and when he heard about the cost, he became upset. He knew right away he couldn't afford to send me there, but he didn't know how to tell me. He'd been making promises for so long.

At the time, I balanced my parents' checkbook,

so I knew how little was coming in each month. Even before Appa told me that he couldn't help me, I had a sense I would never be able to attend UC Davis. However, after the orientation, misfortune struck. I had a major car accident on the freeway after I'd fallen asleep at the wheel. I wasn't seriously injured, but the car was badly damaged.

Appa was furious about the car accident. He never asked me if I was okay. He took away my driving privileges, upset that I had been driving a car at night when I should have been home. After that night, Appa and I grew apart. He didn't trust me, and I wouldn't forgive him for a long time.

Appa was constantly yelling. He didn't let me drive unless it was for school or work, claiming I'd broken our trust when I had the accident. This made me realize I had to leave home.

As I knew Appa wouldn't let me move out to live with any girlfriends or guy friends, I confided my frustrations to Unni.

"Unni, I can't live at home anymore," I told her, "It is impossible for me to reason with Appa. He doesn't trust me."

Unni listened to my complaints for several weeks. During that period, I had a hard time focusing on school. I knew it was hard for Appa to take care of me. I was almost twenty-one years old, and he still had three more children depending on him.

Unni came up with a plan for me to marry her husband's nephew, Calvin. He had a good job and could help support me. When Unni suggested that I marry him, I thought it was odd, but I felt like I didn't have many options. In Korea, girls are not allowed to move out of their parents' home until they are married; it didn't matter if they were 40 years old. At home, it was getting more and more difficult every day to live with Appa. He controlled everything I did; I couldn't talk on the phone, and I wasn't allowed to go anywhere.

I'm sure Appa was just as frustrated. He suffered at the hands of his stubborn pride, and he didn't want to admit that he was losing his daughters.

In the spring of 1990, after one date, Calvin and I were engaged. Appa was furious. He didn't want to give two daughters to one family. I didn't love Calvin, but at the time it was the only way for me to get out of my home. Unni told me marriage is not always about love. She said marriage is about finding someone who will take care of you, and then later you fall in love. I believed Unni, so I married Calvin.

Appa and Umma were upset, but they didn't stop the wedding. I should have told Appa and Umma that I didn't want to marry Calvin, but I couldn't stand living with them any longer. The only way Appa was going to let me leave his home was through marriage. I also didn't want to bring shame to my parents by calling off the wedding.

If I could take those decisions back, I would. I

wish I had been strong enough to simply move out of my parents' house. I knew I wasn't supposed to do it, but it could have saved everyone the suffering that followed.

After just eighteen months of marriage, Calvin and I divorced.

Chapter 29

Moonlight Cleaners

From the time I was ten, I wrote Appa and Umma's checks. I balanced their checkbook each month, made phone calls to their banks and the utility companies, and accompanied them to their doctor appointments to translate their ailments. I even filled in their job applications.

Some times I complained to them about all of these responsibilities. I wanted to talk on the phone with my girlfriends or study my English. However, I knew my parents needed my help, so I tried to do everything they asked. Now, I realize those chores were blessings. I learned to take charge over my life, to deal with the essentials on my own, and to be brave and face my challenges head-on. I became more organized as I had to juggle my personal life with my parents' lives. All of the mail I checked and all of the bills I paid for my parents, prepared me to manage my life and money wisely. I stopped asking for money from Appa and Umma when I was in the seventh grade. I knew they didn't have enough money to pay for my gym clothes, school pictures, yearbooks, and other items. Thus, in seventh grade, I started looking for work.

I sometimes babysat other people's children, but I was never very good at it since I was still a child myself. I didn't make much money, only enough to buy warm clothes for my gym class so that I wouldn't get cold during the winter months.

Starting in seventh grade, I could not see the chalkboard at the front of the classroom. I tried to tell Appa and Umma that I couldn't see very far, but they told me to sit closer so that I could see. At first, I was able to see everything sitting at the front of the class, but my eyes deteriorated further. I decided not to tell Appa or Umma for I knew they were having financial problems.

For a few years, I was not able to see the chalkboard and I didn't learn as much as I should have, especially since I was too shy to raise my hand for help. I focused on helping Appa and Umma with Unni and Jin-bok. Unni went to high school during the day. At night, she went to clean office buildings with other Korean immigrants. On weekends, she cleaned a furniture store near Mather Air Force Base in Rancho Cordova. She met her future husband there when he came in to buy furniture for his new home.

Two years later, Unni was married and living in Elk Grove. She was still in high school at the time. Now, it was up to Jin-bok and myself to help Appa and Umma clean office buildings at night, but Jin-bok was spending less and less time at home. Umma told me that Jin-bok had no interest in helping them; she only wanted to make new friends and have fun.

My three younger siblings, Jin-hun, Jeong-mi, and Jin-suk, stayed home by themselves at night. They did their homework and kept the doors locked. Jin-hun was only ten, while Jeong-mi was eight, and Jin-suk was five. Despite their ages, Jin-hun and Jeong-mi did a good job of watching our baby sister. I think God must have been watching over us because nothing terrible ever happened while we were at work. The younger children kept the house in order and ate by themselves. They had to be brave and work together to keep home life running smoothly.

When I was sixteen years old, I applied for my first job at McDonald's off of Folsom Boulevard in Rancho Cordova. In order to work there, I had to get a permission slip both from school and from my parents. As a minor, I could not work after 10:00 p.m., which I had previously done while helping my parents.

I stopped cleaning office buildings regularly when I got my job at McDonald's. However, I helped Appa and Umma whenever they needed, until I was eighteen and Jin-hun and Jeong-mi began helping them. My youngest sister, Jin-suk, did not work during that time because she was still too young.

Working at McDonald's was a wonderful experience for me. I learned to talk to a wide variety of people. Before that job, I was so shy that I hardly spoke. To this day, I'm not afraid to begin a conversation with strangers. However, I sometimes felt embarrassed when my classmates came in to eat. They didn't make fun of me, but I heard some kids say that they would never work in a place like that. Because of this, I had to swallow my pride.

It was simple work, but it was hard on my legs. I had to stand in one place for a very long time. I came to work on time and left a little later than others. I did whatever the manager asked of me, including cleaning the tables and the bathrooms. I was proud to have a job and my own wages with checks that were in my name. With the wages I received from work, I bought my own yearbooks and school clothes. I even helped my younger siblings buy their school clothes and supplies.

At McDonald's, I learned to use a register, to smile at every person, and to talk to people from all walks of life. As a result, my English improved. Best of all, I learned how to be humble. Today, when I visit a restaurant of any kind, I make sure my children show respect and kindness toward anyone who serves them.

On September 1, 1991, I started my first business. I didn't have any business or managerial education at the time, but had been able to observe Mrs. Overton operate Sunset Cleaners. I watched how she ran her establishment for a few hours, and made mental notes of what I agreed and disagreed with in her business operation.

I was not scared to open my business because I felt

I didn't have anything to lose. I'd had a little experience managing a retail store, and I knew how to design and sew clothes. I could hire and fire people, deposit daily receipts, and organize a payroll. I wanted to open my own custom-design store, but Appa thought I wouldn't make enough money. He suggested opening a pick-up and drop-off cleaners with a focus on alterations.

My landlord, Mr. Mohammed, took a chance on me. He gave me two months of free rent and a two-year contract to lease a storefront. The store was located in Elk Grove, California. A lot of people, including my closest relatives, warned me that I was too young to succeed, but I pledged to work as hard as it would take to help my family financially.

Back at home, our family was suffering at the hands of Appa's gambling addiction. He frequently traveled to Lake Tahoe with his Korean friends to see if he could make money quickly. Umma was forced to work even harder in order to put food on the table, pay rent, and provide clothes for her children.

No local banks would give me a loan without collateral. However, I came across a mail advertisement stating that I was qualified for a $5,000 cash advance at around 22% interest. Subsequently, I requested the loan in order to buy equipment.

I was very fortunate, but it was not easy. I worked seven days a week, twelve to eighteen hours a day. Some days, my clients brought food for me because they could see I worked through lunch and dinner. Shortly after opening, Umma came to help me with my business. My sister Jin-suk helped me after school and on Saturdays. There were a lot of alterations to be done and I did not have enough time to work on my fashion designs. If I had worked on my own designs, the alterations would have piled up; therefore I had to decide what to focus on.

This is when Calvin, my first husband, and I decided to go our separate ways. Calvin was ten years older and wanted a traditional wife who stayed home. I, on the other hand, didn't want to stay home. At 23 years old, I wanted to continue to work and build my business so that I would have enough income to help my parents and my younger siblings. Six months after Calvin and I divorced, I met Rod Nishikawa, my second husband, at the cleaners. Rod was not my client, but he walked into my store one day, asking me to join a local business-networking group. I told him I was too busy to join this club, but Rod kept inviting me until I said "Yes." He even noticed that I worked late every night and didn't eat dinner until after 9 p.m., so he invited me to eat a late dinner with him, stating, "Who else are you going to eat with at this time?" We went on our first date in September 1993, and married two years later.

In 1993, I applied for a loan from a local bank in order to expand my business. I wanted to wash all of the clothes on site instead of sending them out. As I didn't have a written business plan, I had a difficult time receiving a loan.

I worked with my CPA to write the business plan I had in my head, and then I headed to the Union Bank of California because Rod had a good relationship with them. Maria Pasquale, one of the relationship officers, gave me a loan for $100,000 to buy the equipment I needed to open my own plant on site. She was a very kind lady who believed in me, and after nineteen years, she is still my banker.

I think Maria gave me a chance because her upbringing was similar to mine. She was born in Italy, and immigrated to Zimbabwe when she was eight years old. She met her husband in Zimbabwe, and they moved to the United States with their two daughters. At the time, she and her husband only had about a thousand dollars in their pockets and no job prospects. She started with Union Bank of California as a clerk, and then worked her way up to vice president.

After I received my loan, I started to interview

contractors to install the equipment. A man was referred to me by another dry cleaners. He convinced me to hire him, adding that he would buy all the equipment and install it himself.

I did not do a background check. I rushed into signing a contract and paid him $50,000 upfront only for him to deliver a batch of older machines instead of the newer models he'd promised. He never came back to install any of the equipment I'd bought from him. He told me that I was on my own, claiming he was only the salesman. I was upset as I had never before encountered a man as deceitful as him.

Maria had warned me not to pay him. She'd been right, but I'd thought that because he was an old man, he would keep his word. In Korea, a person's word is a valid contract.

He would not give me back any of the money I'd paid up front. My attorney told me that I would spend about $30,000 taking the salesman to court, and there was no guarantee that I would get my money back. I decided not to sue him, instead opting to finish the installation on my own. I needed more money, especially since other contractors told me that the labor would cost more than what this man had previously told me.

I tried to find personal loans from a few people, but no one would help me. I was ready to give up, and because of the stress, I lost a lot of weight, weighing in at a mere 98 pounds. My parents were upset with me, telling me that I was the "trouble maker" in the family. I think they said mean things to me because they felt hopeless knowing they couldn't help financially.

Fortunately, Unni came to my rescue and offered me a loan. She said that she wanted us to be partners. I agreed, knowing she would be a perfect partner since we'd never argued about anything before and I respected and trusted her. She refinanced her home and got a loan for us to finish installing the equipment. The installation was a difficult time in my life, and the entire expansion process drained me of a lot of energy and passion that I had in the beginning. However, after our first month with the new equipment, we made enough for our loan payments. Within seven years, all our loans were paid off.

I met so many wonderful customers at the cleaners, many of whom I will never forget. One customer, Wayne, had a lasting impact on me. He was such a kind man. Once, after work, Wayne drove me to pick up my car at the Mel Rapton Honda dealership where it was getting fixed. It was already seven at night, and it must have taken us 25 minutes to get there, and he wouldn't even take any gas money. While driving, he asked about my background, inquiring about what Appa and Umma did before we immigrated to the United States.

Wayne's family originated in Germany. In the early 1860s, his grandfather traveled across the Midwest on a wagon from Springfield, Illinois, and settled in the Sheldon area near Elk Glove. Something he remembered most vividly from his own childhood was how hard his parents worked and I felt like we connected on that point. I am still grateful for his kindness and his wisdom to this day.

I also grew fond of Mrs. Garcia. She was such a selfless woman. At the time of our friendship, she was dying from breast cancer. However, on several occasions, she would pop into the store just to say "Hello." Some days she would bring me donuts since she suspected I wasn't eating regularly. A few months passed where I did not see her, and I grew concerned. I could tell she had been growing weak, but she never complained. She always greeted the world with a smile and unbending optimism. When I found out she had died, I was deeply saddened. She'd left a husband, a son, and a daughter. To this day, I try to honor her memory by visiting the sick and elderly people in my life at every opportunity. I will never forget Mrs. Garcia's kindness.

I also met a lovely girl, Amanda, at the cleaners. She was just six years old when we met. She came into the cleaners every Saturday with her father, Doug. Amanda had curly blonde hair and beautiful blue eyes. I looked forward to visiting with her each week as she was such a sweet and charming little girl. She is now 28 years old and has graduated from college. We still keep in touch. In the spring of 2007, we took a trip together to South Korea, and now I consider her to be a part of my family.

Another customer, Ben, was a hard-working man. Growing up, his family was very poor, and his parents had many mouths to feed. He came to Elk Grove and started a painting business, working long hours and maintaining honesty with his customers. He was truly a great role model and a wonderful man to know.

Running business isn't easy. Once, I had a customer who brought in a cream-colored skirt for a hem and lining alteration. I hemmed her skirt and used a cream-colored thread to finish the edges. I charged her $12.00, and she picked up her skirt and took it home without any qualms.

The next day, I received an angry phone call from her husband, accusing me of not finishing the hem. I was shocked since I knew I'd done the work and I'd never cheated a customer. The accusation really hurt me. The woman's husband brought the skirt back for me to do it again.

He insisted that I prove I'd done the work. The material from his wife's skirt was in a dumpster outside. Luckily, the trash had not been picked up yet. I felt like I had to prove my integrity, so I climbed into the dumpster and sorted through the trash until I found the piece of material I'd cut from his wife's skirt. I wanted to cry right then, but waited until he left and I could do so in the privacy of my little office. Umma was upset as well.

We also had an incident where we misplaced a customer's suit pants. In order to appease him, we bought him a new suit to use until we located his pants. Eventually, we did find his pants, but he neither paid us for the service nor returned the suit we'd loaned to him. He didn't realize how long Umma and I had to work in order to make up that lost money. Luckily, we didn't have many customers like him, or I don't know what we would've done. I might have lost faith in people.

It all worked out in the end. Most of my customers were honest and kind to Umma and me. If things weren't ready on time, most people were very understanding. My cleaners was not just a place to drop off clothes; it was a place to talk about weddings, spouses, births, deaths, children, and more. Because of those friendships, my life has become so much richer.

I look back in amazement at how a small business could have grown into so much. I had the right sort of support and guidance, especially from Umma. She had preached to be honest with my customers and bequeathed her sewing skills unto me. Even greater, Umma lent me her strength, her wisdom, and her generosity. She would tell me to check each piece of clothing for quality, making me sew any torn seams. Our customers may not have noticed some tears if it had not been for Umma's diligence. Umma's advice to cherish our customers yielded a happy and fruitful business.

Eventually, it was time for me to let go of the business and start a family. I sold my half of the business to Unni in 1997. From then on, I dedicated my time to my second husband, Rod and our three beautiful children. My greatest passion is to make sure our children grow up to be loving, kind, and honest people, and I have succeeded thus far.

Chapter 30

Embracing Two Cultures

Today I feel fortunate to live within two different cultures. The path I've chosen has had its challenges and its blessings, but with patience comes wisdom. I realized I could not prevent myself from embracing both my Korean and my American identity. Neither wholly defines me. The path toward my identity is an unfinished one.

When I first started school in 1978, the English language sounded like indistinguishable noise to me. Still, I had a strong desire to make American friends. I may not have known the word for "friendship," but I still managed to form those bonds. I played with all of my classmates regardless of their appearances. Some of them had blonde hair and blue eyes, while others had curly hair and dark skin. Even my own cousins had physical characteristics I'd never seen before. However, all this didn't keep me from loving them equally.

There are some subtle cultural differences between Koreans and Americans. Some Americans do not take their shoes off when they enter their homes or bedrooms. That was a shock for me to see because at my house, we never wore shoes into our bedrooms. Also, Americans don't bow their heads when greeting someone as they do in Korea. American children are not responsible for the same show of respect for their parents or elders as are Korean children. In American households, the youngest person eats first while the oldest male eats first in Korea. However, these are only practices that define our histories, not our value as individuals.

After I joined the International Club at American

River College, I knew being a Korean American was something to be treasured. I was the only Korean American in the group. There were people from Germany, Spain, Poland, France, Peru, Columbia, Argentina, Czechoslovakia, Jordan, Iran, Ethiopia, India, and the Philippines. It was like the United Nations. Once a month, we got together at someone's home and just had a good time. We didn't compare our cultural differences, instead focusing on what we had in common, learning to trust one another, and building friendships.

I decided in the seventh grade that I would focus on the similarities instead of the differences in all of us. We all have the same desires for education, health, happiness, safety, and peace.

Today, I try to greet as many people as I encounter and learn as much about them as they care to share with me. I think it is only the fear of the unknown that keeps one group of people from understanding another. The way we look and dress may separate us temporarily, but when you take the time to get to know a person, you realize how much that person has in common with you.

Having friendships with people of different cultures can invite so many new possibilities. There is a wealth of colors and flavors beyond the culture into which you are born. Having friends from so many different countries and ethnic backgrounds invites only blessings into one's life.

When I was a child, I thought being rich meant having fancy cars, a big house, and expensive clothes. As I grew older, I realized that those are just temporary materials on the path of one's life. You cannot find true happiness in what you wear. Being truly rich is to give love generously and to allow yourself to receive it. My soul is awake at this moment, and for that, I feel eternally rich.

Afterword by Dr. Heather Sellens

Author Jeannie Johng-Nishikawa first wrote her memories of growing up in South Korea and her family's emigration to Northern California as a bedtime story for her three children. In *Dreaming in English*, Johng-Nishikawa describes in detail how her family struggled to survive the post Korean War destruction and managed to find happiness in simplicity. Her story portrays a picture of enormous human spirit and optimism.

I was astounded reading about her family's thatched-roof home, with no electricity nor water, and the struggle to gather enough food for the day. I read how a body is prepared for burial, Korean folk medicine, pregnant women's taboos, the naming systems, family connections and even the remarkable "on-dol" heated floors in every Korean home, rich or poor. It is incredible to see how quickly Korea has grown from the country of Sami's childhood to the influential country of today.

The second half of the book is Sami's memory of her new life in America. Sami and her parents leave every day, and everybody, behind in Korea for a better opportunity they hope awaits them in California. Her parents worked long hours at multiple jobs, with Sami working alongside of them, even cleaning offices on school nights. She struggles first to understand the language in school and then to participate in typically American schoolgirl activities. The description of her first ice cream cone is genuine. Mint chocolate chip!

The pressures of immigration and language difficulties were not easy for her family. Sami and her siblings soon realize that the U.S. is full of unexpected language barriers and bi-cultural confusions. They tried to imitate American peers, though their wary parents refused to accept anything but Korean behavior. Her parents had major misgivings when Sami wanted to attend a weeklong school outing. In the book, the only way Sami was allowed to have a relationship with a man was to get married. The marriage failed, but her newfound freedom opened up huge possibilities for Sami's business, education, and eventually new love and marriage.

The book is easy to read (8-9th grade level) and Sami's language immerses the readers into the lives of the 1960's Korean culture. My university Multicultural Children's Literature class enjoyed her book very much, and many of my students told me how they had experienced the same difficulties when they came to the U.S.

I would recommend *Dreaming in English* for parents and teachers looking for a good book about immigration, cultural assimilation, and hope. Readers will come away with a new awareness of the needs and challenges of immigrants and the abundance we Americans take for granted.

—Dr. Heather Sellens, California State University, Sacramento,

Multicultural Children's Literature Course

Glossary

Ajuma means aunt or older married woman with children.

Appa means Father. It is used especially by young children.

Bo-ri-cha is barley that has been roasted in a black metal pot and boiled to make tea. It is delicious to drink when you don't feel well, especially during winter months. Bo-ri-cha helps ease diarrhea and vomiting.

Boochimgae is a type of pancakes made from many forms of grain and vegetables.

Cham-weh is a Korean melon that is yellow on the outside and white inside. It's very sweet. The seeds are also edible and delicious.

Halmoni can be used in reference to your grandmother or anyone who is an elderly woman.

Hanbok is traditional Korean clothing made from hemp and silk fiber. Today hanbok is made from many other fibers, including polyester and nylon.

Hangari is made by potters who use a special firing technique. Kimchi, soy sauce, red pepper sauce, and soybeans ferment at just the right temperature inside these earthenware pots.

Hangul is Korean alphabet. It was invented in the fifteenth century by King Sejong to teach common citizens to read and write.

Hanji are very beautiful papers made from mulberry bark. The papers can last for many generations.

Han River is the 4th longest river in the Korean peninsula.

Harabaji means Grandfather.

Ingeolmi are rice cakes that are covered in soybean powder.

Jin-dal-lai is a flower that comes from the Hibiscus family. It's pink in color and smells sweet and sour. You can sometimes eat the flower but you must be careful to make sure it is safe and clean. Umma used Jin-dal-lai for making special beers and wines in Yesan.

Jook is rice porridge.

Keun Umma means Big Mother.

Kimchi is made from Napa cabbage with red pepper paste and many other ingredients like garlic, radishes, green onions, and fish sauce.

Komo is in reference to your aunt on your father's side.

Komobo refers to an uncle-in-law from your father's side that is married to Komo.

Ko-sa-ri is a fern that glows in the woods or mountains. It's green when fresh, and when picked and dried it becomes brown. Many Koreans pick ko-sa-li during spring. It can be dried and stored to be eaten during the winter.

Kwi-Shin means ghost.

Makgeolli is fermented Korean beer made from rice and wheat.

Mandu are pot stickers.

Mujigae-tteok are rainbow rice cakes with many different layers of colors from natural ingredients. Only salt and sugar are added.

Nuruk is yeast.

On-dol is a type of floor and heating system to keep the rooms warm during winter months. The heat can simultaneously be used for cooking.

Oppa refers to an older brother, usually used by a younger sister.

Seoul is the capital of South Korea.

Songpyeon is a half moon shaped rice cake that's served during the fall Thanksgiving celebration. It comes in many colors and is usually stuffed with beans and sesame seeds. Now, songpyeon is served for other occasions, like weddings, funerals, and even births.

Seonbi refers to a scholar or teacher.

Suk is mugwort herb that can be used as a medication for treating infections or used for food dye or fiber. It is highly fragrant.

Tteok is a rice cake that's made from sweet rice. There are many varieties of rice cakes.

Tteok gouk is rice cake soup eaten on New Year's Day. However, tteok gouk is eaten just about any time now both in Korea and in the U.S.

Umma means Mommy, Mom, or Mother.

Unni refers to an older sister.

Yangban refers to a noble person, female or male.

Yi is a family name. Also used in reference to the Yi Dynasty that ruled Korea from (1392-1910). Yi is also spelled Lee or Rhee.

Yo-gang is a chamber pot used during the night since we didn't have indoor toilets on our farm.